#QuietingTheSilence: Personal Stories

THE BLUE DOVE FOUNDATION

Published for noncommercial, charitable use by the Blue Dove Foundation Inc. For reprint or redistribution requests, please contact the Blue Dove Foundation Inc. To order books or inquire about bulk sales, visit www.quietthesilence.org

First Edition and First Volume
Amazon ISBN Number 9781077509443
Independently published with Amazon

Distributed by:
The Blue Dove Foundation
1200 Ashwood Parkway, Suite 400
Atlanta, GA 30338
www.TheBlueDoveFoundation.org
Info@TheBlueDoveFoundation.org

Sheri Panovka, editor & writer
Denise Cowden at Brilliantbox, designer

TABLE OF CONTENTS

ABOUT THE BOOK

Nearly one in five Americans eighteen years and older experienced mental illness in 2018, according to a report by the U.S. Department of Health & Human Services. About one in five Americans older than twelve used an illicit drug, which includes misusing prescription opioids. Substance abuse was more common among both adolescents and adults who had a mental health issue.

If you are Jewish, there's a good chance you're thinking these statistics don't apply to you. For a long time, many Jews refused to believe these problems exist in the Jewish community. Even today, the shame and stigma that persist keep people from speaking out and seeking–or offering–help. But as the stories in this book reveal, Jews are as likely as anyone else to be affected by mental illness and/or addiction.

These personal stories come from the heart and soul. Some of the stories may touch you directly or remind you of someone you know who has gone through a similar experience. We hope you find them meaningful and encourage you to share the book with anyone who may benefit from it.

If you start to feel overwhelmed while reading, close the book and try taking some deep breaths. If you need immediate assistance, **call 911** or the National Alliance on Mental Illness (NAMI) at **1.800.950.NAMI (6264)**. You can find additional national hotlines in the resources section of this book.

ACKNOWLEDGEMENTS

We wish to express our utmost gratitude to the courageous individuals and families who opened up their lives to share their very personal stories and show others with similar stories they are not alone. They exemplify the meaning of #QuietingTheSilence and the importance of working to eliminate the shame and stigma associated with mental illness and addiction.

A big mazal tov to the team that worked so hard to create #QuietingTheSilence: Personal Stories. When dedicated people with a true passion for tikkun olam work together, anything is possible.

- Alyza Berman Milrad, Justin Milrad & Daniel Epstein, founders of the Blue Dove Foundation
- Gabrielle Leon Spatt, executive director of the Blue Dove Foundation
- The Blue Dove Foundation Board of Directors, Board of Advisors & staff

ABOUT THE BLUE DOVE FOUNDATION

Who We Are

The Blue Dove Foundation was created to help address the issues of mental illness and substance abuse in the Jewish community and beyond. Based in Atlanta, we work with people and organizations across the United States and around the world.

The Jewish community is not immune to the problems the rest of society wrestles with when it comes to mental health and substance abuse. Yet we as a group too often have refused to acknowledge and discuss the issues. As a result, many individuals and their families suffer privately and lack the information necessary to address their struggles.

Recognizing the importance of collaboration when it comes to solving this community problem, we accomplish our work through program, promotional, and support partnerships. The Foundation values both our existing relationships and future partners whose missions align with ours.

Our Mission

To educate, equip, and ignite our Jewish community with tools to understand, support, and overcome the challenges presented by mental illness and substance abuse. As a community with a focus on tikkun olam, we work to eradicate the shame and stigma surrounding these issues. Once we achieve this goal, we can begin to improve and save lives.

Our Work

1. Education, awareness, and outreach: We encourage conversations and provide information and tools for individuals and families seeking assistance.

2. Financial assistance for treatment: We provide hardship scholarships and/or interest-free loans.

3. Scalable programs: We develop, design, and launch easily replicated programs for schools, synagogues, community centers, camps, institutions, and affinity groups. Programs include speaker series, mental health Shabbat dinners, community trainings utilizing the Blue Dove Foundation Mental Wellness Toolkit, and more.

Why the Dove

In the book of Genesis, Noah released a dove after the great flood in order to see if the water had subsided. It came back carrying a freshly plucked olive leaf (Hebrew: עלה זית alay zayit), a sign of life and of God's bringing Noah, his family, and the animals to a renewed land.

The dove represents peace of the deepest kind. It soothes and quiets our worried or troubled thoughts, enabling us to find renewal in the silence of the mind. Its roles as a spiritual messenger, maternal symbol, and liaison impart an inner peace that helps us go about our lives calmly and with purpose. Some believe the dove also represents hope, while others believe it denotes freedom.

Bringing peace, life, hope, and freedom for those facing addiction or other mental health challenges is the goal of the Blue Dove Foundation.

@ TheBlueDoveFoundation   @BlueDoveFoundation

www.TheBlueDoveFoundation.org

WHY #QUIETINGTHESILENCE

The Blue Dove Foundation created #QuietingTheSilence as a platform to help individuals and organizations create programs and events focusing on mental health and substance use. Our goal is to offer members of the community a chance to come together to share their own experiences in this arena.

We have found that hearing personal stories of struggles and loss directly from those living through them makes a stronger impact and helps foster new perspectives, personal connections, ideas, and hope. The narratives that follow come from individuals with a Jewish background who have gone through a life-changing experience, either personally or through a loved one. By sharing them, we can show others with similar stories they are not alone and begin to eliminate the shame and stigma many feel when it comes to mental illness and addiction.

We know accomplishing that goal will take time. It isn't easy to speak out publicly. You will notice several of the stories come from people who wish to remain anonymous. Ideally, everyone would be comfortable sharing his or her name, but not everybody is ready. That's OK. Telling their stories at all is a start, and the more we talk more about these issues, the faster we'll get there.

We encourage you to continue sharing your own stories and your reactions to the stories in this book on social media. When you do, please include the hashtag #QuietingTheSilence in your posts.

If you are interested in hosting a #QuietingTheSilence event in your community, additional tools and resources are available at theBluedoveFoundation.org. Or reach out to us at info@thebluedovefoundation.org.

MAKING AN IMPACT

How can you #QuietTheSilence and continue to engage with others in mental health conversations?

You do not need to be an expert to make a significant impact. You just need to be caring and informed. But you also should be aware of your limits.

One of the greatest impacts you can make is by becoming an ally–to your friends, to your family, and to your community. Let others know you are there for them as they seek help. Continue to educate yourself about mental illness and addiction. Consider taking classes if they are offered locally. Identify and familiarize yourself with the different local and national hotlines and resources available to help.

Most important, don't be a bystander. If you believe someone is struggling, reach out. Your spouse/child/parent/loved one/friend needs your support more than ever, and it will make a huge difference.

When we work together, we can contribute collectively to transforming the culture of the Jewish community, so people feel safe and enjoy a sense of belonging. By demonstrating a willingness to both offer and seek support, we can help tear down walls of shame.

FOREWORD

I have a little story to tell about an instructive experience I had around forty years ago. One night my late wife, Penny, told me our neighbor had poured her heart out to her that day. "Hannah" and her husband "Morris," a middle-aged Jewish couple, had built a home across the street from us a year or two previously. Hannah told Penny their youngest son, "Allen," was a heroin addict. He was living out of state and recently had been hospitalized, again, for rehab after being arrested, again, for drug-related charges. At the time, I was in recovery from codependency, a disorder involving the emotional cost of having a loved one who suffered with an addiction of one sort or another. My first wife had been addicted to pills and alcohol. I became severely depressed as the quality of my life deteriorated and despaired that anything would ever improve. At the time, I knew little to nothing about these things, including the fact that she was addicted. I just thought she was mentally ill. As our marriage ended (thankfully for both of us), I was fortunate to meet several people in Alcoholics Anonymous and Al-Anon who were kind enough to share the experience, strength, and hope that had brought them into recovery.

One of the most remarkable things about these people was their honesty. I had always lived by the code that you had to pretend you were fine (my family was perfect, we had no problems or personal shortcomings, imperfections were found in other people, and so on…). But in these Al-Anon and AA meetings, I heard people talking about their fears, resentments, selfishness, and the like. The others in the room accepted them for who they were and confessed they could relate. This was immensely freeing for me—a young man who had put a tremendous amount of energy into acting as though I was fine and paying a high price for it. When the truth of my life was revealed to me, I became involved in Al-Anon, even though my marriage had ended. I applied the principles of the twelve steps to my daily life and experienced a spiritual awakening. I also transitioned my medical practice from family to addiction medicine.

It was in this context that I heard of the plight of my neighbors. I invited Hannah and Morris to go with me to my weekly Al-Anon group. Morris declined, but Hannah agreed to go—reluctantly. We met at a Lutheran church on a Saturday morning. I thought the meeting was a good one. Driving home afterward, I asked Hannah what she thought. She said she was uncomfortable going to a meeting on a Saturday morning at a Lutheran church, where at the end of the meeting, everyone said the Lord's Prayer. She never went back. On the one hand, I thought she was making excuses for not wanting to deal with her own codependency, because she was far from an observant Jew. But on the other hand, I thought she had a valid point. Where was a Jewish place where a Jewish person could get help of this type? I decided at that moment if I ever had the opportunity to facilitate a twelve-step group in a Jewish place, I would do so.

Around this time, my own drinking was becoming habitual. A few days after my fortieth birthday, Penny confronted me about it. I thus had to admit to myself I had secretly been concerned about my drinking for some time and decided to quit. I joined AA, and, thank God, I have not had a drink since. When we moved from Madison, Wisconsin, to Marietta, Georgia, in 1984, we joined Temple Kehillat Chaim. At that time, we did not have our own synagogue building. We subsequently acquired property in Roswell, where we remain. After we built our social hall/education building in 1996, I approached Rabbi Winokur and the board about opening our facility to an AA group. They supported the idea fully, and we had our first meeting in June 1996. We have met every Tuesday night since, unless the date conflicted with Rosh Hashanah or Yom Kippur. The meetings are open to the community at large. While there is no question that at least a few Jewish people have come because they occur in a Jewish place, I am equally convinced other Jewish people have stayed away for reasons of privacy. Almost never have the Jewish attendees outnumbered our non-Jewish friends, but I am rarely the only Jewish person there. I am proud of my temple for openly embracing this group.

In early 2003, I again approached the board and Rabbi Winokur about sponsoring an event. I would be sixty years old and twenty years sober that

March and wanted to have a big birthday/recovery party. We combined the event with our annual choir festival, and I hired a local comedian for entertainment. We sold tickets and raised $5,000 for the temple. More than 150 people attended this Jewish celebration of sobriety. I was very proud of everyone and grateful I could be an agent of education to the reality that we do have addiction in our community. It is important to acknowledge it and vital to openly celebrate recovery. We quieted the silence, at least for the night.

In the pages that follow, you will read stories of courage, faith, and heart-breaking loss. The writers have openly shared their deepest, most painful emotional struggles with their own mental illnesses and addictions, and those of their beloved children, siblings, and parents. Not every story has a happy ending, but each carries a message of hope. We tell our stories so others will summon the courage to face their own painful circumstances and seek the expert help that is now much more skilled and available than in the past. I am humbled to have been asked to participate in this project with these honest and brave people. And I am hopeful something in these stories will give readers the impetus to make a decision, if necessary, to get the help they need for themselves or for a loved one.

I commend the Blue Dove Foundation for its commitment to breaking down the barriers of shame, fear, and ignorance, so our entire Jewish community can accept the challenge of being honest about the addiction and mental illness that exist in our own stressful world.

Michael Gordon, MD
Medical Director, the Berman Center

Dr. Gordon graduated from the University of Illinois College of Medicine in Chicago with a specialty in family medicine. Early on, he realized his calling was addiction medicine. His passion is working with patients who are willing to be honest with themselves and who are ready to make positive changes in their lives.

Prior to his current role, Dr. Gordon served as medical director of adult addiction services at the Brawner Psychiatric Institute in Smyrna, Georgia; was on staff at the Ridgeview Institute in Smyrna; and ran a private outpatient practice.

"Wellness is the complete integration of body, mind, and spirit—the realization that everything we do, think, feel, and believe has an effect on our state of well-being."

Greg Anderson
Wellness Author & Speaker

SHARING THEIR PERSONAL STORIES

This book was created for the community by the community. All the individuals who shared their experiences have released their stories and personal identifying information to the Blue Dove Foundation. We encourage people and organizations to share these stories. Written permission must be secured from the Blue Dove Foundation to use or reproduce any part of this book, except for brief quotations in reviews or articles, or links to stories online.

If you share a story online, please visit our website and link to it directly. All stories listed in this book can be found at quietingthesilence.org.

If you share on social media, please be sure to tag us on Facebook (@TheBlueDoveFoundation) and Instagram (@BlueDovefoundation). We also ask that you use the #QuietingTheSilence on all social media posts across all platforms.

If you have any questions about sharing these stories, please contact us at info@thebluedovefoundation.org.

HER HIDDEN STRUGGLE

My younger sister, Sari, and I grew up in the affluent, tightly knit Jewish community of Coral Springs, Florida. We were raised with strong family values and were lucky to spend a lot of time with our grandparents, cousins, and a large group of very close family friends. Overall, even with our parents' divorce when we were in elementary school, we had a very normal American upbringing.

But as Sari got older, coping with the day to day was difficult for her. In high school, she finally was diagnosed with bipolar disorder, and like many others who suffer with this disease, she cycled through medications, treatments, and therapists. Treatments would help for a few months and then suddenly wouldn't. Different triggers would set her off. Little issues became big ones, and she met them with screaming, insults, and sadness. Faced with constant frustration at herself, she started looking for other ways to be happy, including occasional drug use.

When things were good, she was good. Really good.

Unable to help herself, Sari responded outwardly by devoting her life to helping others. In college, she volunteered with children who had autism and eventually earned a master's degree in sign language education. She was teaching third grade, and both the students and their parents talked about how much she cared for them. She even made YouTube videos translating popular music into sign language.

When things were good, she was good. Really good.

At thirty years old, Sari had touched many lives for the better and seemed to have kicked her bad habits. To others, she presented a warm, nurturing young woman. But when things got bad in her mind, coping without drugs must have seemed an impossible task.

It was our grandmother who found her. Hurricane Irma was battering Florida, and Sari had lost power, so she went to stay with our grandparents. After spending a wonderful day together cooking and grading school papers, she was set to spend the night. Later that evening, Grandma heard her on the phone having a tough conversation and then heard the front door close. This call obviously had been a trigger for Sari. Looking in the hall, Grandma realized she was gone.

"We're in the hospital. Sari overdosed."

When Grandma called her cell, Sari said she just had to run an errand and would be right back. She returned about midnight and immediately went into the bathroom. After about 10 minutes of silence, Grandma knocked. No answer. She opened the door and found Sari hunched over, barely breathing. She called 911. Can you imagine a ninety-year-old woman doing CPR on her granddaughter? The ambulance came, and the EMS team administered Narcan before rushing her to the hospital. (If you don't know, Narcan is a medication used to block the effects of opioids, especially in an overdose.)

When my mom called me early that morning, I knew something was wrong. But I expected it to be about my grandparents, who were ninety and ninety-nine. I never thought it would be the news she shared: "We're in the hospital. Sari overdosed."

I immediately booked a ticket and flew home, and for the next several days, I don't know how we survived it. Why did this happen? We had so many questions. How did we not know what she was doing?

We do not believe Sari intentionally took her life. After losing a dear friend years ago, she said, "I wouldn't kill myself." I don't want people to experience how I feel now." And there was no way she would do it at our grandparents' house. She loved them so much. But likely unknown to her, the drugs she took were laced with fentanyl, a powerful and dangerous additive, and the drug became a game of Russian roulette.

She never regained consciousness. After several days and yet another brain scan, there was minimal brain activity and no improvement. She was living only because of a machine, and my family had a tough decision to make—one I don't wish on my worst enemy. Eleven minutes after she was removed from the ventilator, she was gone. It was crazy to experience. You never think this could happen, but it did. Things can change very quickly.

Sari died on September 14, 2017, from a heroin overdose. Even worse, she wasn't the only one. Within two days of Sari's death, twenty-one other people in South Florida of various ages died from fentanyl-based overdoses.

...and the drug became a game of Russian roulette.

So here we are two years later. Sari is buried with our other grandparents and a dear friend who also struggled with mental health. Her headstone is simple yet descriptive: Daughter, sister, granddaughter, friend. A menorah and a playing card. She was buried in the dress she was going to wear to my wedding, which was four months after she passed away.

At Sari's funeral, we talked about how she struggled at different times in her life. We did not say she died from an overdose at the funeral, but most people there knew. It took me six months to tell people outside of my inner circle how she died and to share my story. How do you talk about it? There is a stigma attached. Today, I feel comfortable saying it. I think it just took time. But back then, I couldn't even focus on what happened.

Mom wasn't ashamed. Our community knew she had a daughter who struggled with mental health. She talks about it today, and she's OK. She's stronger than we all imagined. My father, who lives far away, connected with other parents on Facebook and locally who have suffered through the same thing. My step-father suffered a stroke shortly after Sari died and is talking about it too. We couldn't have gotten to where we are today without that same wonderful community of family and friends who supported us so much growing up and supports us just as much today. They never cease to amaze me by showing up with food, stories, and big smiles.

I'm less of a talker and more of a doer. I have taken every opportunity I could to make a difference in an area that needs so much work. I immediately started volunteering. It helped me with my grieving process. Being involved and trying to make change happen is the only way I know. Today, I am the executive director of the Blue Dove Foundation. I see daily how much connecting with people means and how many people are looking for light.

I have learned a lot over the past few years. I learned that in this national endeavor to fight opioid use, recreational users often get overlooked. I learned how tightly mental health is connected to drug abuse. And I learned it can happen to anyone—even when you come from a nice Jewish family. We as a society have made a lot of progress, but there still is so much room to grow. I learned help is out there through various organizations and a wealth of people; you just have to ask. And we need to talk more. We as a community need to quiet the silence that surrounds the issues of substance abuse and mental health overall. I hope you and others will join me in the conversation.

- GABBY SPATT

BOUNCING BACK FROM MY ROCK BOTTOM

I was adopted in March 1980, and my folks split up a couple of years later. Each remarried in 1984. My dad, who was part Jewish but did not grow up religiously, did not go down a Jewish path. My mom married an Orthodox man, who I called Abba, and decided to raise my brother and me Jewishly. Since I was very young, religion was a point of contention and something with which I struggle even today.

We moved to Potomac, Maryland, in 1987. My mom and stepfather decided to follow the Orthodox tradition, and I ended up at an Orthodox day school in third grade. As I got older, I never fully felt like I fit in. I wasn't good academically or socially. I didn't really know where to land. In high school, I had only a few friends. Some fit into the standard norm of an Orthodox Jewish kid, some didn't. I seemed to be drawn to bad behavior, even though that wasn't how I was raised. I guess because I didn't feel like I fit in, I decided to act the part.

The one thing I knew for sure was I wasn't happy. I didn't put forth any effort in school or try to achieve anything. Looking back, I realize I didn't have any faith in myself to try anything.

I think I was thirteen when I tried smoking pot. I didn't get high and didn't do it again for a few years. I also got really drunk for the first time, at a New Year's party. Being dumb and clumsy was comical to me. I really enjoyed it, and over the next few years, I got drunk whenever I could.

I started smoking pot more often when I was about fifteen. My friends and I would get high on weekends and sometimes at school. Then one day in January 1997, these kids from an alternative high school came to give us the 'Drug Talk'. Afterward, one of my classmates sent an anonymous note to the guidance counselor saying he (or she) was concerned after seeing me drunk. The school called my parents and recommended I call one of the girls who spoke at the school to see if she would be willing to take me to a twelve-step meeting. So that Superbowl Sunday, I was in Alcoholics

Anonymous. The meeting was at a clubhouse in a smoky room. I wanted to fit in, so I smoked a cigarette (and started a habit that lasted fifteen years).

Although they wanted me to stop using and get on to a better path, my mom and Abba were not happy about AA. The meetings had me associating with non-Jewish kids they didn't like. Rather than being able to focus on recovery, I always felt like I was doing something wrong. Once again, religion became the center of every argument.

A few months went by, and I just seemed to be getting worse. I was really unhappy. I felt like I didn't fit in with my new friends or belong at the Jewish school. There seemed to be nowhere to go. My parents were always disappointed in me; I couldn't do anything right. I was depressed and anxious, but everyone just thought I was a bad kid. It got to the point where I wanted to disappear.

One day in April 1997, I wrote my best friend a note that I was going to kill myself in the yard at school. I told her to have someone come look for me after lunch. I knew something had to give and didn't know how to get someone's attention. After the suicide attempt, I was admitted to the psychiatric ward of a local hospital for a few days for deep intensive therapy. The day I got out, my mom and I were called into the school headmistress's office.

I will never forget that day. My mom, who was progressively losing her vision from a degenerative eye disease, had to ride with me into school. It was us and this headmistress. No guidance counselor. She referred to me as a 'freak' who didn't fit in with the standard kids at this school and informed us they were expelling me. They kicked me out a few weeks before the end of my junior year. I had been there nine years. This was how they dealt with mental illness in 1997 at an Orthodox Jewish high school in metro D.C. True, I was not a good student. But they expelled me for trying to *kill* myself. It was devastating. I felt horrible. My parents were crushed.

I ended up going to the high school that came to speak to us. I went from being the bad kid in a Jewish environment to a sheltered kid in an alternative school. Another place where I didn't fit in. It wasn't long before many of my friends were not allowed to hang out with me anymore. I am still grateful for all the open-minded and loving families that always accepted me into their homes despite my reputation. I don't know if they will ever understand how much that meant to me.

I had spent most of high school planning to study in Israel the year after I graduated. After my expulsion, though, most programs there wouldn't accept me. But one awesome rabbi heard about me and was still willing to have a conversation about it. Within two hours of meeting, he accepted me, and a few months later I was off to Israel.

Almost immediately, I began drinking and drugging. A lot of people get there and party for a month or two, and then stop. I just did not stop. I went from drinking and smoking pot to doing ecstasy almost every day. I began dealing drugs and living a pretty dangerous lifestyle in a foreign country. The most interesting thing about that year was that despite the drugs and everything else, it was the first time I found a core group of people I fit in with. It was a good feeling.

When I left for Israel, I planned to come home and go to the University of Maryland. But after spending the summer at home, I enrolled at Touro College in New York City. I moved into a dorm in September 1999.

I don't know how I functioned. I was always high or drunk. Thinking back, it was miserable. Still, it was my life. When you're on ecstasy, everything is great. But when you're on it for so long, it becomes maintenance. It's like you can't be happy unless you're high, but the high doesn't last long, so you are constantly chasing it. Yet you never find it. I feel like I spent the better part of a decade in a comedown. Needless to say, I was not doing well in school. And once again, I was the bad kid.

I don't know how I functioned. I was always high or drunk.

And then in 2001, 9/11 happened. I was living in the dorm on West 85th and Amsterdam. That morning, someone came running into my room and told me about the plane. I ran through the dorm to find my close friend Devora. Her brother-in-law had been in the Twin Towers and was missing. I found her in the dorm mother's apartment in the middle of girls all praying. We hugged. I don't remember saying anything, just the hugging. I felt helpless and useless, so I got into a cab with another student and told the driver to go south. After registering with the Salvation Army as volunteers, we were put in a van and driven to Ground Zero. I could never come up with words for the things I saw, smelled, experienced. It was just *remarkable*—one of the single greatest tragedies our country has experienced, and I was standing right there giving water to those who were picking up pieces of rubble, hoping to find people. It made a mark on my soul that forever changed me.

Another friend and I went later to the West Side Highway, where volunteers were giving out drinks and supplies to first responders as they came out of the wreckage. I don't know how these responders kept going in. That day I developed a love for police and firefighters.

Finally, we knew we had to go home, where I proceeded to drink myself into oblivion. That picked up my drinking quite a bit and led to my willingness to try cocaine.

I finished college in 2003, moved back to Maryland and got my first job, working in a nonprofit. I had the potential to be so good at what I was doing and even got promoted. But I spent so much time out drinking and doing drugs that I was always hung over or still drunk or high at work. I spent all my money on drugs and alcohol. I faked injuries so I could go to the hospital, and insurance would pay for opioid pain killers.

My next job ended after only a year. I had officially become unemployable. I ran out of money and had no place to live. I called my brother and sister-in-law to ask them to bail me out of a financial bind, and they did the best thing anyone could have done: They said no. I think they were starting to realize what was going on and understood that enabling me would have been the worst thing they could do. It probably saved my life. I went to visit them around that time and was so worn out that I couldn't enjoy time with my niece and nephew. I just wanted to be high.

In February 2006, I moved back in with my parents. I had spent so long buying other people drinks and drugs, because that was the only way I thought people would like me. But when I had no money, nobody was buying me anything, so I had no access to drugs and alcohol anymore. I was either going to have to start doing things for drugs and alcohol, or I was going to get clean. It was a horrible place in life. I felt alone. My family was so disappointed in me. I couldn't land a job. I was just a mess.

Then one day I admitted to my parents I was using, and we decided I would start going to twelve-step meetings again. Going to the first meeting gave me the courage to tell my mom details of what I had been going through. For the first time, she really understood how bad things had gotten with my drug use. It was also the first time I was honest, fully and completely. We agreed if I stayed sober and went to AA meetings, I could stay in the house. If I relapsed, I would be out.

 **That was my rock bottom.**

I stayed sober for five and a half months, during which I found a job. And then a girlfriend and I decided it would be fun to go out dancing. It was the dumbest thing I could have done. I was drunk and seeking cocaine within an hour. My parents made me find a new place. I moved into a sober home and stayed clean for about fifteen months. Pleased with where things were going, I moved into my own place—and relapsed immediately. It was a horrible three-week relapse. It wasn't the quantity of drugs or alcohol. It was the behavior that went with it. I stole from my family and alienated everyone. I'll never forget the morning of March 10, 2008. My grandma called me and said, "I know you stole money from me." I'll never forget the sound of her voice. She had just buried her husband of sixty-six years, my grandpa. That's where my addiction took me. I stole money from my grieving grandma, who I loved with all my soul. Even though I did worse things, that was it for me. That was my rock bottom. I haven't had a drink or a drug since that day.

One of the biggest gifts I found in sobriety—and there were many—was time with family members who have died since. I spent a beautiful seven years with my grandma, who passed away being proud of the person I had become, having forgiven me for all of my mistakes. My stepmother died about the same time, and I had been able to make amends to her as well for past transgressions.

As I started to come out of the fog of addiction, I came to discover (contrary to the little voice in my head for so many years) I was actually quite a talented professional. My career took off, and I started to achieve things I never thought possible. I started giving back to my community instead of mooching off it. I also became active in the recovery community, which has been a source of joy and sadness. The painful reality is you are going to lose people to this disease. But you also get to watch people celebrate their first year clean.

In April 2012, I called my mom and told her I really loved my life as a single and successful professional, and I didn't think I wanted to get married. She cried. Then, two weeks later, I was playing softball in a sober league, when I met this adorable man named Bart. He had been sober for a year. To my mother's relief, we married eighteen months later. I gave birth to my first child, Elianna, in December 2014 and then to my second child, Sophia, in February 2016. Sophia was named for my grandma, who passed away while I was pregnant with her.

My beautiful and courageous mom died in 2017 after battling uterine cancer that metastasized to her lungs. I was able to spend a lot of years with her clean. She was at my wedding and met both of my children. I was able to make amends to her. We had a remarkable relationship that was both funny and honest. I asked her before she died if there was anything she thought was left unsaid between us or anything she felt I needed to atone for, and there wasn't. It was one of the many gifts I received because of my sobriety.

Today I take things day by day. I still struggle with depression and anxiety, but I know how to advocate for my own mental health now. I still have cravings, but I also have the tools to work through them. I went from being dishonest about everything in my life to being an open book when anyone asks. I like talking about my sobriety, because it takes the stigma out of it. Addiction happens—even in the Jewish community—and it's something we all need to talk about.

Today I take things day by day.

For the last few years, I have been asked to speak to the school that expelled me in 1997. The guidance department developed a program to deal with issues like addiction and mental health. I am honored to support that effort. It shows the tide is changing with regard to how our community talks about these issues.

When our kids are older, Bart and I want them to know where we come from. How we will handle that, I don't know. I don't know yet what it's like to be the parent of a teenager. I want them to be comfortable talking to me in ways I wasn't with my parents. I want them to feel safe and tell us everything. It scares the heck out of me. But I also know that God or the universe or whatever there is out there hasn't gotten me this far to drop me now. We'll figure it out.

- MICHELLE DAY

OVERCOMING ADDICTION

It all started when I got arrested for shoplifting in February 2012, about three months before my high school graduation. I had a lot going on emotionally and had done some stupid things that led to my taking a mental health break from school and starting an outpatient treatment program.

A few days after the arrest, I snuck onto school property in the middle of the night. I remember it was a Tuesday. There was no good reason; it was just something to do. And part of my entitlement attitude led me to believe I had a right to sneak onto our school's roof, where there was an amazing skyline view. The same night, the school was sprayed with graffiti. I didn't do it, but I got the blame. (Years later, some kids from a different school would confess to it.)

The next day, while I was in my outpatient program, my parents (my mom and stepdad, who raised me) were called into school and told I was not allowed back. I found out when they came to pick me up. I can't tell you how humiliating it was. And as a part of being expelled, the school strongly encouraged them to send me to inpatient treatment. (By the way, I was the third kid to get kicked out and put into rehab that year.) So instead of going home, they took me straight to another facility. I was the youngest person in this program—not quite eighteen. It was a halfway house where we had group therapy daily, attended Alcoholics Anonymous meetings nightly, and lived with therapists who provided twenty-four-hour counseling. It was there that I was informed I was a drug addict. I fought that diagnosis. Yes, I was smoking marijuana daily, but I honestly didn't consider myself an addict. I had done LSD once and ecstasy twice, but that was the extent of my drug use.

I left the inpatient program in May 2012, around graduation time. I didn't get to attend the graduation ceremony, although I did receive my diploma that October. I was completely sober from drugs at this point. I was living at home, waitressing and attending Narcotics Anonymous (NA) meetings every night. I was still drinking, though; in my mind, I never had a problem with alcohol.

At the same time, I had been having panic attacks about never being able to smoke weed again. It was a medicine for me. I lied in NA about my drinking. I was drug free but still drinking. I continued to pick up my chips marking my sobriety. I didn't feel bad about lying. I was told I was an addict and had to live sober or would be institutionalized. My parents put this persona on me, and I had to live up to it. I really felt it was a survival thing. If my parents knew I wasn't sober, I wouldn't be able to finish high school or live at home. I had to lie, so I didn't feel guilty at all. I just didn't drink at home. I drank after work but made sure I was sober when I went home.

Why did I relapse like that?

On my eight-month anniversary of being drug free, I smoked weed again for the first time since treatment. This was October 2012. Having graduated high school, I was planning to start college the following January. I didn't think smoking weed would lead to a downward spiral. I spent eight months in NA and drank the entire time. When you're in NA, you're supposed to hang out with others in NA. When I got out of rehab, I continued to hang out with them and proceeded to try the drugs they did.

Why did I relapse like that? I think in part it was because I felt really unheard and alone, and like nobody understood me. I was being told I had a diagnosis, and because I was under eighteen, I felt I couldn't stand up and say it didn't sound right. And, of course, every addict in treatment says that.

In December 2012, I was arrested for DUI.

A month later I started at Georgia State as a film student. My parents thought if I moved into a dorm, it might put me on the right path. So I did, but I didn't know anyone there and felt so alone, anxious, and depressed—even though I was studying what I wanted to and had everything paid for. I was looking for some kind of escape. I didn't talk to my parents about my feelings. I didn't think they would know what to do with that idea.

Then one night in February 2013, a boy from rehab texted me and asked if he could stay on my couch. He had been kicked out of his apartment, because his roommate found syringes. He had heroin with him, and I asked if I could try it. I was hooked by the third time I did it.

For the next year and a half, I did heroin every day. I dropped out of GSU and got a refund on my tuition—without my parents' knowledge. I took the money and bought enough drugs to last me about six weeks. I pretended to go to class every day. I also applied to Savannah College of Art & Design (SCAD) in Atlanta. During that time, I introduced heroin to my best friend, Maddie. I wanted her to try what I had fallen in love with, so I bought her a small bag of the substance. We would snort it for fun. About a year into my heroin use, I met a boy and fell in love. He taught me how to use a needle.

When you do heroin for about three months, you get to a state where if you're not giving it to your body, you go into withdrawal—like a flu times ten. That's when all hell broke loose. I started breaking into my parents' house, writing fraudulent checks, shoplifting, stealing food to eat as well as electronics to pawn, and spending all my money on heroin. It was a quick progression.

My parents knew. There was an incident when I was parked in front of their house and fell asleep with my head on the steering wheel. A neighbor's kid saw me and thought I was dead. I woke up to firetrucks and police at my car window. My parents took me to a drug testing facility not accessible to MARTA. They expected me to fail, but I faked the drug test and passed it. Still, they didn't believe me when I said I was not on drugs and put me back into rehab. They gave me an ultimatum: either treatment or a one-way MARTA ticket. It was tough love.

I decided to go to treatment. I moved into a residential program for three years. You'd form your own halfway houses with others in rehab. The first year, I cut everyone out of my life who was not in rehab. I cut out all my friends I was shooting heroin with, including the boyfriend who gave me my first dose. The only person I refused to cut out of my life was Maddie. She would visit me in treatment and pick me up after my group therapy sessions. I started living cleanly. I didn't realize how miserable I had been until the end of my initial intensive forty-five days. I started feeling happier again and more like myself. When I came into rehab, I had been living out of my car. I never ate, so I was impossibly skinny. Before, I woke up every day thinking about who I would steal from. I had a $150-a-day habit and no job. Now, I was waking up not feeling sick or wondering who to steal from. I fought really hard to never get back there again. I still do.

Six months into treatment, I got a call that Maddie passed away from a heroin overdose. During the last conversation we had, she told me she wanted to get sober, but her parents just didn't have the resources to put her into treatment. Around the time Maddie passed, SCAD responded to my application. I had been accepted. I started college again a few months later, in 2015.

I had a $150-a-day habit and no job.

I have buried a lot of friends, and I carry a lot of guilt. The guilt from Maddie's death really helped to keep me sober. I attended fifteen funerals in the first three years after rehab. The oldest was twenty-nine; the youngest, seventeen.

And then I guess it got to the three-year mark, and everyone I got high with was either dead or in recovery—except for the boyfriend I had fallen in love with while I had been using. He had been in prison. The check fraud I committed caught up with him, and he had a few run-ins with the law following that. After about three and half years in recovery, I reached out to him. I heard he was out of prison, and I wanted to make amends for the part I played. We reconnected and figured out we still had feelings for each other. Three months later, he relapsed on heroin and never woke up from his high. I was completely devastated. That was another big factor in keeping me sober. He died on December 3, 2017. It was close to my four-year mark of sobriety. That was probably the lowest I had ever been. I tried to get heroin again. I wanted to kill myself with it, because all my friends had died. I hit up five or six people. Not a single person got back to me. All were either dead or in prison. I got through that deep grief and haven't wanted to use a substance again. His passing is what closed that chapter of my life and started a new chapter one.

A few months after he died, I graduated from SCAD and had three job offers. I fought really hard, pulled myself up, and made a conscious decision I wasn't going to kill myself. Heroin used to be something fun, and now it equals suicide in my mind.

Today, I don't consider myself either sober or a drug addict. I don't want to put a label on it or put myself into a box. I stay away from opioids. I'll have a half glass of wine once in a while. I don't go out to bars with friends; instead, I stay home and watch TV most nights. I spend a lot of time with my parents. There is still a lot of pain and hurt and rebuilding, but we have built a strong, loving relationship. I have a great job and can pay for my own place, which I share with two little bunnies.

I like to volunteer my time, and the biggest part of my service work is sharing my story. I go to my old school and others, and I work with addiction programs. I don't want other people to go through what I did. If I can save someone else that pain, that would be cool. If I have one message, it's to be honest with yourself. Don't cover up your feelings; reach out. Grasp onto support. Just being aware of your emotions makes a world of difference.

I don't give myself rules to live by other than living honestly and treating everyone with love and respect.

- BELLA

I DIDN'T CAUSE IT, I CAN'T CONTROL IT, I CAN'T CURE IT

I am a sixty-year-old Jewish doctor, and my daughter is a drug addict. I'm happy to say she's alive and thriving, but not too long ago, I was afraid I would have to prepare myself to bury her.

When my daughter, Bella, was midway through twelfth grade, the school counselor called me into a meeting. She had been skipping classes, and they suspected drug use from what they were hearing. We put a tracker on her car and phone, we questioned her, we grounded her. Before I could figure out what to do next, she was arrested by city police for shoplifting. Then, by the end of that week, she got kicked out of high school for vandalism.

It was a wakeup call. Before all this happened, I have to admit I was in denial. I believed my daughter was struggling just like all teenage girls do. Now I was scared to death and found it hard to wrap my head around what was happening. She had been seeing a psychiatrist and taking meds for ADHD her whole life. She had been in counseling since my divorce when she was young. She was in a private school with accommodations. I had been doing everything I knew to do. In truth, I was angry I had to deal with this drug problem now too.

When Bella was released from jail, I took her to the local public psychiatric hospital. The doctor recommended out-patient care at first. Once she got kicked out of school, they directed us to a ninety-day rehab program. I searched online first, not knowing what to look at. I was lost and so confused. I ended up sending her to a program they recommended.

At the same time, the hospital counselor said something very important: Addiction is a family disease, and I needed to go to Al-Anon.

Going to Al-Anon then, and still going now, has changed my life.

I had no understanding of the disease of addiction, how we got here, what to do now. I was scared to death, anxious, guilty, and ashamed. Most of all, I was confused about what to do next. Who could I talk to? My parents blamed my parenting, my rabbi had no suggestions, my friends gave me advice that was all over the place. I could barely sleep or work. I was so distracted.

Addiction is a family disease, and I needed to go to Al-Anon.

In Al-Anon and a family recovery program, I came to understand my parenting did not cause this. There were working moms and stay-at-home moms; kids in public school and homeschool; wealthy and working class; permissive parenting and restrictive. We were all in the same boat. I was able to let go, over time, of my guilt and shame. I did grieve, though, for the illusion I had of my child, the dreams I had for my child's life.

I faced the fact that addiction runs in our family, so she is genetically predisposed. Her poor self-esteem issues and anxiety led her to self-medicate. She never felt like she fit in. She felt emotionally abandoned by her father. The circumstances of my divorce created stress in her life, and her wiring led her down this road. In high school, her friends kept changing. She spent more time alone in her room, and she wouldn't talk with me anymore. These were the circumstances of her life. I was doing the best I could. I was not to blame. I had no control over her choices.

I learned this child needed to be parented differently than the others. When my daughter slid back and deeper into drugs, shooting heroin at college a year and a half later, I was better prepared. Denial was still there, until it got too crazy. Coming home with the flu every few weeks, which I now know is opioid withdrawal. Having her things stolen or lost, which I now know were traded or pawned for drugs. Finding things missing from our home, like jewelry and cash. Frequent car accidents and blowing out tires.

Being lost or abandoned at night in bad neighborhoods and calling for a pickup.

With suggested resources from other Al-Anon parents, I was able to choose a recovery program I believed could help us—the Insight Program, an Enthusiastic Sobriety program with locations in Georgia and North Carolina. With the support of its staff, my husband and I confronted our daughter. I had no control over her behavior, but I had choices about mine. I came to believe that anything I provided to my daughter to keep her safe—a meal, some cash, a bed—actually was contributing to her using drugs for one more day. I could not keep her alive. She could overdose up in her room as well as out on a street.

I finally chose tough love, because I could not live with the daily dramas and anxiety. We took her phone and her car, which belonged to us, changed the locks on the house and gave her the choice of rehab or a bus pass. Her choice was help or homelessness. She knew I was serious this time. I had defined my boundaries for my mental health. I couldn't take the craziness any more.

She chose help. She was belligerent and defiant. The drugs were in her system for months, distorting her thinking. The pain and anxiety she had been numbing out with drugs were in full force. She had a tough road to recovery. We emphasized she had to choose the life she wanted for herself. We couldn't live her life for her. She made that journey and is the wiser for it. She understands her struggles and where she gets tripped up, and she has tools and strategies to cope. She found through the recovery community she was loved for exactly who she was no matter how that looked.

The wisdom, faith, sponsor support, and tools of the twelve-step program of Al-Anon got me to this point of influence in my daughter's life. I had to let go and get out of her way. I had to have faith that a loving God was looking out for her, that she has her soul's journey to make. I learned loving detachment. I learned to live in the moment, not futurizing disaster that might not come or rehashing past moments with guilt or shame. I learned to take care of myself emotionally and spiritually. I learned to be grateful for

I learned to take care of myself emotionally and spiritually.

what was and appreciate the small daily miracles. I learned to live my life joyfully, regardless of my daughter's choice. I found a community of parents who understood and did not judge me by her actions.

Teasing out what is parenting and what is enabling my child was the most difficult lesson I have ever had to learn. This has led us both to be independent of each other yet have a close adult-to-young adult relationship we both treasure. She can call for advice and then choose to do what she wants. My happiness is not dependent on her actions.

Bella has completed college and is working in an industry she loves. From completing the twelve steps, I am emotionally and spiritually healthier than I've ever been. I am happy and content in all aspects of my life, whether there are challenging circumstances or not on any given day. We have grown our souls through this journey.

- BELLA'S MOM

NOT WHO YOU THINK

As a society, we have an idea of what a drug addict is supposed to look like. But as my story demonstrates, no one is immune to this disease, regardless of your background, how much money you have, your intellectual ability, or how loving and caring a Jewish mother you have.

I'm twenty-eight years old as I write this, and I'm a recovering drug addict. As a child, I had everything I ever needed and pretty much everything I ever wanted. I have two loving parents who have been married thirty years, an older brother, and a younger sister. I never experienced any significant trauma people sometimes think is a prerequisite to having substance abuse issues. I was a fairly outgoing and popular kid with lots of friends, and I played just about every sport growing up. I did well in classes; was student body president of my elementary, middle, and high schools; got a perfect score on the math portion of the SAT; was in the honors program at a top state university, where I graduated with honors; and eventually went on to law school, again graduating with honors.

I'm twenty-eight years old as I write this, and I'm a recovering drug addict.

I'll skip elementary and middle school, because nothing too exciting happened, and fast forward to ninth grade. My parents sent me to a small, private Jewish high school, which was quite a change from the large public schools where I had been, but I liked it. I didn't know anyone when I got there, but within two weeks I was hanging out with the older kids and smoking weed. I went from trying it the first time to smoking every weekend to smoking every day, multiple times a day. I went from zero to smoking pot in people's cars and thinking I was invincible pretty much overnight. And this is an important detail. Substance abuse is a progressive disease that, when active, always gets worse—and worsens more quickly—as time passes. Whenever I tried some new drug I liked, my use would escalate over time. And each time I got sober and then relapsed, I hit the ground harder and faster than ever before. The whole idea that taking a break for some period of time would "reset the clock," so to speak, is just simply not the case.

Most of the rest of my high school years were seemingly "normal" when it came to my drug use—or so I thought. I tried cocaine a few times, had a handful of psychedelic mushroom trips with some friends, shared a couple of Percocets when my friends or I got our wisdom teeth out, and so forth. I think it's safe to say that up to this point, I enjoyed getting drunk and high, but it in no way consumed me.

During my senior year, I became full-on hooked. I was introduced to OxyContin, which is basically the same chemical as oxycodone or Roxicodone. From that first time I tried a "roxy," I wanted one badly every day. As was the case with my pot smoking, what started with one pill a day quickly turned into an expensive and potentially lethal daily habit. As my pill use increased and became more expensive, I did what pretty much every other prescription pain pill addict who lives long enough does. I turned to a cheaper and stronger alternative: heroin.

As I mentioned, I managed to make it through college with honors, and it was precisely at this time that I turned to heroin. So again, I'll remind you to really reconsider what you think a drug addict is supposed to look like. Not many people think of heroin addicts as well-off suburban white kids who are on full rides to college and had just been offered a full ride to law school. Around the end of my junior year, my parents caught wind of what I was doing. My best friend had been caught by his parents doing the same stuff. Knowing he and I hung out all the time, his parents decided to call my parents and basically say, "Here's what our son has been doing. We know he and your son hang out, so you may want to talk to him."

By this point, getting high wasn't even remotely fun anymore. I would wake up feeling like I had the flu every morning. I was constantly broke, no one trusted me, and I could be in a crowd full of people yet still feel alone.

Every night I would go to sleep promising myself I would never do this again, and every morning I would wake up feeling like getting out of bed was impossible without my fix. So even though I may have looked much different than that heroin addict living under some highway overpass downtown, I can assure you I felt every bit as bad inside. So when my parents sat me down, I decided to come clean.

After the initial relief I experienced from being honest wore off, I spent the next couple of months faking my way through therapy and cheating drug tests. That eventually caught up with me, and after my last exam of my first semester of senior year, I drove straight to a rehab center and checked myself in. I was twenty years old and gung-ho about turning my life around. But my story is not all rainbows and unicorns from here.

The hardest part for me was asking for help.

Following treatment, I moved into a sober living facility, and after about six months there, I relapsed. This started my tour of sober living facilities in the area, as I bounced from place to place: six months, relapse, nine months, relapse, one year, relapse, eighteen months, relapse. While that sounds like a pretty miserable existence, a lot of good came out of each of those experiences. First, I proved to myself I was much happier and productive when I was sober. Second, I learned my loved ones only wanted what was best for me and would be there to support me no matter what. And most important, it proved setbacks happen, and it's okay as long as I get back up and keep trying.

The hardest part for me was asking for help. Each time I relapsed, I knew my friends and family would be eager to help me if they knew I was struggling. But I felt ashamed and embarrassed, saying to myself, "Look at all this stuff I have around me. I'm not supposed to feel this way." Yet if there's one thing that is perfectly normal for a drug addict to feel, it's the feeling of wanting to get high.

This inability to ask for help kept me out there risking my life every day trying to get high. My best friend, the one I mentioned earlier, also struggled with asking for help, and that struggle cost him his life. We were at Gozapalooza, I think it's called—the party on Christmas eve that all the Jews go to, because we have nothing else to do. Instead of talking to some girls like we were hoping to, he and I spent most of the evening near one of the corners talking to each other. He was dealing with some stress at work, he had accepted a new job and was worried about telling his current job he was leaving. Meanwhile, he had gotten another job offer he liked even more and was weighing how to tell the company with which he had just accepted a job that he had changed his mind. He didn't tell me these decisions were starting to take a toll on him, and despite having been sober for quite a while, he wanted to quiet the noise in his head. He wanted to get high, and even though he knew I was sober and had been through many of the same struggles, he found himself unable to ask for help. He felt it was wrong that he was having these thoughts and was disappointed in himself for having them—even though he hadn't acted on them. So he didn't say anything.

Two days later, I got a call around eight o'clock in the morning from my roommate's mom. All she said was "Go home." And without her saying anything else, I knew he was dead.

I share my friend's story for a few reasons: He was the only person I knew who used drugs the way I did, and his story is yet another reminder of how lucky I am to be alive. A lot of people say things like, "All it takes is that one time, and it could be too late," but you never think it will happen to you. At least I didn't. At his funeral, his family spoke openly about his struggles with addiction, which taught me how powerful just talking about our struggles can be. I can't tell you how many people have opened up about their own battles after hearing his. They wanted to know what to do for their son, daughter, husband, wife, friend, whoever. I don't necessarily have the magic answer, but what we can do is talk to the people around us. We need to normalize the idea that we all have challenges. I'm not knocking Facebook or Instagram or anything like that, but they definitely put pressure on all of us to portray this image that everything is great all the time. And, in today's day and age, face-to-face conversations seem far less common. I'm guilty of it as much as the next guy; I'm always glued to my phone. We need to take the time to remind the people around us we care and are there for them, whether they are struggling or not. Even though my best friend knew it, I wish I had reminded him when we last spoke that I would always be there for him, no matter what. That I cared.

 # We need to normalize the idea that we all have challenges.

As part of my recovery, I find it important to give back and help others struggling with alcoholism and addiction. Aside from the inherent difficulty of asking for help, a lot of people don't, because they feel like they can't afford it. And loved ones don't offer the help, because they don't know what to do. If you know someone who is struggling, reach out and help them. All you have to do is start the conversation.

- AN UNLIKELY ADDICT

OVERCOMING MY EATING DISORDER

Let's start with dieting. We've all been there. Wanting to lose a few pounds, trying some quick fixes, growing more and more frustrated when the weight comes back. Sound familiar? If you answered yes, then you probably know: Being on a diet is not fun. "A diet" could mean anything from restricting certain food groups to avoiding social situations to becoming obsessed with counting calories and limiting fat.

There's a fine line between dieting and disordered behavior, and it gets crossed all too often. In fact, according to the National Eating Disorders Association (NEDA), more than thirty million Americans will struggle with an eating disorder at some point in their lives.

Being on a diet is not fun.

The dieting industry is a multibillion-dollar business. It works hard to convince us we are not good enough, so we'll buy into weight-loss products. More often than not, whatever diet we invest in fails, and we gain the weight back. Who feels better at the end of this?

Soon after I turned fifteen, the dieting industry won, and I started my first commercialized weight loss program. I had gained a little extra weight during my adolescence (as many girls naturally do) and decided I wanted to lose ten pounds. Little did I know, my innocent diet was about to turn into a rollercoaster of disordered eating.

Trigger Warning*

Ten pounds quickly turned to twenty pounds, and just like that, I had developed every symptom of anorexia nervosa. Within a year, I had lost more than thirty pounds. With that weight loss, my metabolism slowed, I lost a great deal of muscle, developed low bone-mineral density, and never had an appetite. Oh, and my menstrual cycle stopped.

Yet, the compliments were rolling in. "You look amazing," was a message I heard over and over, and interpreted as "you used to look fat." So I kept restricting. My mind was fixated on calories, and nobody could understand why.

I didn't realize under-eating had an impact and was inflicting consequences on my health. My body had gone into a fat-preserving zone, and I had become deficient in vitamins and minerals my body needed to function. Even though I had achieved my weight-loss goals, I certainly was not happy. My brain could not think about anything but food. *What did I eat at my last meal? What did I plan on eating next? Did I need to cut down on a certain food group?* I was always cold and tired. Eating out became a stressor. I even remember crying while on vacation after learning sugar-free ice cream still contained calories. Seriously, who wants to live like that?

Even though I had achieved my weight loss goals, I certainly was not happy.

At my annual checkup, my doctor noticed I had lost a significant amount of weight. Instead of referring me to a therapist who specialized in eating disorders, she told me to come back in a week so she could continue to monitor my weight. The unfortunate truth was that my doctor was doing what she thought was best.

Healthcare professionals receive minimal training in eating disorders and holistic health in medical school, and yet situations similar to mine are far too common. In fact, physical weight is not always a predictor for an eating disorder. There are many cases where individuals maintain a higher weight and still struggle with anorexia nervosa and associated disorders.

One day, I said to hell with restricting, and I began bingeing. I had turned a full one-eighty. I trained my body to eat even when I was not hungry. After being deprived for so long, my metabolism was out of whack, and I began gaining weight quickly. To me, gaining weight was better than constantly obsessing over calories, so I kept eating. With time, I had changed my neural pathways to eat out of every emotion that was not hunger. This is referred to as binge eating disorder. My doctors were concerned with the weight gain and misdiagnosed me with polycystic ovarian syndrome, also referred to as PCOS. They treated me as a prediabetic rather than an individual with an eating disorder. Thus, disordered eating became my new normal.

I began to relearn nutrition my junior year of college. I was taking health and wellness classes at Binghamton University, where I learned to view food as fuel and physical activity as strength. I learned about Health at Every Size® (HAES) and Intuitive eating (IE). My classmates began to speak openly about their personal battles with food, and I saw my story wasn't unique. It was actually pretty common. With time, I began changing my behavior and started loving myself enough to live a healthy lifestyle.

But I was not healed. For years afterward, I thought I had found recovery in college. I was so very wrong. I was brainwashed by society into thinking counting calories and excessive cravings were "willpower issues," and my higher weight was a reflection of my "lack of self-control." I was lying to myself, and I was lying to everyone around me. I continued to believe struggling with my weight was something I would have to do forever. Until I relapsed.

When I moved to Atlanta in September 2017, I relapsed so badly I had no choice but to ask for help. I went through five therapists until I found somebody who could really help me navigate recovery. Many clinicians told me they specialized in eating disorders, but I was continuously triggered by their practices. *(It is important to ask your clinicians if they use an HAES and IE approach.)*

Once I finally found the right one, we revisited many pieces of my past. I realized that while I had been learning about intuitive eating in college, I also was learning about body composition and weight management. I was receiving mixed messages about what it meant to be healthy. I know now health is not correlated with weight, and beauty is only a construct of society. There is nothing wrong with being fat. It is society that gives fat a negative connotation.

I learned to focus on my behaviors rather than the number on the scale. I learned about the power of self-compassion, and nourishing my body with fruits, veggies, ice cream, and pizza was essential to a balanced life. I learned physical activity was not about calories, weight loss, or bikini bodies; rather, it was about pushing myself because I was worth it.

With my therapist, I visited past traumas. I allowed myself to take the power back and to stop internalizing difficult situations. I also learned how to identify when other people were projecting their own insecurities onto me. Not only did recovery give me my life back; it brought me a better life.

Today, I classify myself as an individual in long-term recovery. I do believe in full recovery from an eating disorder. With that being said, it is not linear, and lapses happen along the way. I have decided to be honest with myself and allow a few years before I identify as being fully recovered.

My final words to you are, the struggle is so very real, and it's OK. You are not alone. But if you are struggling, please ask for help. You are worth a life filled with love, belonging, purpose, and self-compassion. You deserve to be happy.

If you are experiencing symptoms similar to what I mentioned above, help is available. Call the NEDA helpline at (800) 931-2237.

I recognize that eating disorders are a social justice issue, and it was a privilege to receive adequate treatment. I use my recovery story to advocate for change. I have lobbied for eating disorder legislation and have educated individuals from healthcare providers to senators on the impact and mortality rate of eating disorders. I hope that one day, nobody will ever have to struggle with an eating disorder again.

Dear E.D.-

Thank you for allowing me to find a community of people who have provided hope and inspiration. Thank you for showing me life is so much better without you, and prioritizing myself is not selfish but necessary. Thank you for showing me I am strong and resilient. Thank you for allowing me to create a career that inspires people to fight back against you. I needed something as awful as you to show myself there is beauty in life.

Sincerely,
Me

- JOCELYN RESNICK, MPH CHES

ME, AN ADDICT?!?

In the fall of 2010, I enrolled in a clinical pastoral education course as part of my rabbinical training. We watched films about addiction, which the instructors introduced by inviting us to pay attention to the questions the addicts were asking. I heard their pain, isolation, shame, and desire for a better life. I listened as they asked if they were doomed to their fate. Did they deserve their suffering? Could they live without their substance of choice? Would they ever find happiness and inner peace?

I understood for the first time addicts aren't just people in movies or begging on the street corner. I'd been asking myself those same questions for many years. And I realized I—a rabbinical student and a mensch—am an addict.

What does it mean to be an addict? How could this happen? Why did it take thirty-one years to see the truth about myself? Could I find healing? Dare I believe the future could be better than the present?

Growing up, I never learned about addiction. My father was a rabbi, my mother a Jewish day school teacher and principal. We moved every few years because of their work. My mother had significant medical challenges and was in and out of hospitals my entire life. My parents' marriage was far from perfect, and I lived in fear of having to move again. I was always afraid Mom would get sick, Dad would lose his job, or they would yell at me for something I did or didn't do. While my parents clearly loved me, I rarely felt loved, secure, or safe, and had no outlets to process my difficult upbringing.

Mom was a professional baker on the side, and one thing she taught me was there was no problem that couldn't be solved with the right amount of sugar. From early on, I learned to drown my emotions with cookies, cakes, pies, and ice cream. I'd finish everyone's leftovers, because children were starving in Africa, and it was a shame to waste food. I gained weight and was ridiculed for doing so. I felt worse about myself, and the only solution I knew was to eat more. I didn't know I was an addict. I just knew if I ate enough food, somehow the pain I was feeling would disappear, at least for a bit.

I also picked at my skin, pulled at my eyebrows, chewed on my cheeks, and bit my nails. Once I started, I often couldn't stop, even when I did damage to my skin. I wet the bed frequently, was overweight, and had asthma, sleep apnea, and an irregular heart rhythm. I struggled to focus in school, developed significant learning impairments, and had no one to talk to about it. My role at home was to take care of my mother and siblings. I learned to cook, clean, and do laundry from a very young age. My mother made it clear she didn't have time to deal with my challenges; her own were more important. Why couldn't I just get myself together already? Maybe these struggles were my fault. Maybe I deserved to be yelled at. If I behaved better, they'd have no reason to yell at me, right? If only I did better in school and managed to always anticipate everyone's needs around the house better, I'd be okay. That's what I told myself anyway.

I didn't know I was an addict.

In middle school, my classmates started dating. I was petrified anyone I asked out would discover how miserable I was. Mom told me my job in life was to find a nice Jewish girl who was doing good work in the world, put her on a pedestal, and give her everything she wanted, because men were jerks. How would I find the right one for me? What would I say to her? She never explained, and I was petrified to ask.

When I discovered pornography in eighth grade, a lightbulb went off in my head, and I became addicted to that too. I pretended the women in the magazines were attracted to me. They didn't judge me or make me feel bad. I stole magazines from the bookstore (I couldn't possibly pay for them; someone could see me, I'd be found out, Mom would scream at me, Dad could get fired…).

I wanted my mother (and everyone else) to like me and was always seeking validation. I couldn't express emotions. I was afraid they wouldn't be heard or, worse, I'd be ridiculed for even having them. I spent hundreds if not thousands of hours playing solitaire, minesweeper, and other free games. When I won one, I felt like I was accomplishing something. Unfortunately, that feeling never lasted. The next game was always calling me.

In college I heard about Hazon, now the largest Jewish environmental organization. Its first event was a bike ride from Seattle to Washington, D.C. I felt called to participate and spent ten glorious weeks riding across America. I learned I was capable of accomplishing big things. I discovered a sense of God and holiness in the outdoors that has stayed with me until this day.

I also started dating and almost married my first love. When I was with her, I felt safe and secure, like I could finally breathe. The moment she left the room, I was alone with myself, feeling as miserable and worthless as ever. When she called off our engagement, I was heartbroken, even as I knew it needed to happen. I became a Jewish environmental educator with Teva, and for the first time, I had a community where all parts of me could exist at once. My fellow staffers were incredibly supportive, and I loved teaching in the outdoors.

After two years, I was called in a different direction. Mom had been waiting for her second liver transplant, and my grandmother was taking care of her. Savta needed a break, so I became Mom's caregiver. She had the transplant but lost a lot of blood, ending up in intensive care for two months and then the hospital and rehab for another two before she could go home. She was never strong enough to go back to work, and except for a few weekends when family or friends would visit, I couldn't leave her. I was twenty-seven when she died. My life was in shambles. I had no energy to do anything except eat my way through my emotions. There wasn't enough food to fill the sadness inside me.

Eventually, I was ready to reenter the world. I went to rabbinical school, yearning for community and hoping to find answers to my prayers and guidance for the way forward. I studied at ALEPH: Alliance for Jewish Renewal with founder Reb Zalman Schachter-Shalomi and others there and throughout the Jewish world. I spent a year in Jerusalem, learning at the Pardes Institute and drumming with Nava Tehila, a music-infused spiritual community. The Torah was inspiring, the community supportive. And still, I was looking for my bride. I thought I'd find her in Israel. If only...

I moved back and became rabbi of a synagogue in North Bergen, New Jersey. The people were nice but two or three times my age. Living in a small room in the back of the synagogue, I was lonely and bored. I ate all the Kiddush leftovers (and then some) and watched too much television and pornography. I did good work, but I had no friends.

I started dating a rabbinical student, making the two-hour drive to see her regularly. This was when I discovered I was addicted to food. She introduced me to a functional medicine doctor, who took me off of flour, gluten, sugar, and dairy. Sigh.

We got married, and I was ordained as a rabbi. She finished a few months later, and we moved to Memphis to co-rabbi at a synagogue. We didn't work well together. The job was all encompassing, and the honeymoon wore off shortly after we arrived. I thought if I followed my mother's advice and gave her everything she wanted, I'd be happy. Alas, I was miserable and couldn't understand why.

I started to see a therapist, who sent me to the Healing Trauma Program at Onsite retreat center. I learned about childhood trauma, attachment, bonding, addiction, codependency, and more. I realized I wasn't just addicted to food. I had a lot of work I needed to do, but I knew I could do it.

Soon after the retreat, on December 19, 2014, I was in the Memphis Public Library's used bookstore, perusing the addiction section. I purchased Pia Melody's *Facing Love Addiction* and read it in two days. I understood I had been using pornography as a way of self-medicating and masking my

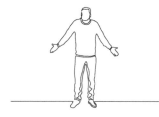

Alas, I was miserable and couldn't understand why.

emotions. I consider that to be Day 1 of my sobriety and haven't looked at pornography since. I wish I could say my other addictive behaviors have been as easy to stop. Thank God I found a sponsor and started working the twelve steps shortly after that. I read a lot of books, listened to recovery podcasts, and participated in many meetings.

My marriage wasn't strong enough to survive. My ex left town, and I stayed at the synagogue on my own. The work was hard, and I committed to my recovery. I hired a trainer at the JCC and started working out three times a week. I ate a lot better and worked with an emotional healer, a life coach, and a therapist. I talked regularly with my sponsor, and spoke monthly with my spiritual director. It took a whole team to keep my head in the right place (and it still does!).

I wondered what else was out there in the Jewish world. I connected with Beit T'Shuvah, a residential addiction treatment center and congregation, and took part in its educator training. I found only a few books on Amazon and very little online. I wondered why we don't have a real national movement to address recovery in the Jewish world. Why aren't there more Jewish books, podcasts, coaching programs, cruises, Facebook groups, and opportunities to learn and grow?

Meanwhile, I started dating someone long distance and made the difficult decision to leave Memphis. I moved to Silver Spring, Maryland; married my wife, Sherri; finished a coaching certification; launched Torah of Life, a motivational Jewish podcast; and was ready to take on the world. Unfortunately, I learned my father was dying of lung cancer. I put my work on hiatus to be with him. I was sad when he died, but I'm glad that instead of drowning my feelings in food and pornography, I shared them, went to meetings, and used the tools of the program to process my grief and loss, and find healthy ways to move forward.

I know my parents loved me and did the best they could. I'm grateful for all they taught me, even as I wish life could have been different. And yet, had I had a happier childhood, I might not have discovered the calling that has become my life's work.

I created Our Jewish Recovery to be a home for Jews recovering from addiction, their loved ones, and Jewish educators. The Facebook group is growing, the resources on the website are expanding, and people are sharing their experience, strength, and hope one day at a time. I published a book to show Jews can be addicts, and there is no inherent conflict between recovery and a commitment to Jewish life. Addiction is not new in the Jewish world; stories go back thousands of years, and I believe Judaism has spiritual tools that can be of assistance to anyone working on sobriety. I wrote the book I wish I could have read when I was in early recovery. I also became a family programs facilitator with Shatterproof, a national nonprofit focused on addiction, training people on how to address the consequences of their loved ones' addictive behaviors. I work with rabbis and other Jewish educators and am slowly building a movement of healing.

It's time to end the stigma of addiction in the Jewish world. We struggle with it like everyone else. And we can heal as well. I am a testament to that. My recovery isn't perfect, and my life isn't either. I can tell you, though, the worst day of my life today is so much better than the best day I had in active addiction. I am happier and freer than I've ever been, and I'll do my best to help others find those blessings as well. We all deserve peace, joy, love, connection, and a community that lifts us up. I hope and pray we will be that community for one another. Together, we can be a light of healing throughout the Jewish world, so everyone touched by addiction can find happiness, holiness, healing, and peace. May it be so.

- RABBI ILAN GLAZER

CONFESSIONS OF A DERMATILLOMANIAC

For years I thought I was alone in a freakish existence. I guess we—those of us living with mental illness—all start out that way until the day we finally discover we aren't alone at all. Or freakish. We're just human.

I began picking my skin when I was six years old. I remember that first manic episode well, because it was the day my mother was hauled away in an ambulance after the first of many overdoses to come in the years ahead. My childhood was clouded by my mother's mental illness (close to six diagnoses to date) and her invasive addiction to prescription pain and sleep medications. Then alcohol. Then back to medication.

Fortunately, I was a child who had supportive grandparents who were able to raise me in their home and take care of my mother under their roof. They tried to hide my mother's addiction, but because I was forced to grow up too quickly and always be on high alert, that was impossible. I had no choice but to survive in a house that was constantly in a war zone of my mother's creation. No one could shield me from my parent's divorce, my father's abusive nature, or my mother's addiction.

I began picking my skin when I was six years old.

Growing up in a dysfunctional home of addiction, divorce, and mental illness was a hard burden to bear. Starting in elementary school, I felt the pressure from my grandparents and my own anxious mind to hide my secret home life from the world. I naturally fought to fit in with my peers, prove myself to my teachers, and show everyone I wasn't anything like my mom.

Education was my escape from the hell I was living. I threw myself into school as early as first grade, never accepting anything below a B on report cards. As a child completely helpless about my home and family circumstances, I desperately searched for anything I could control. Grades fit that bill. I had complete power over how hard I worked and became one of the top students in school. I coped with my home life—a present reality I couldn't control—by knowing I could construct my own future.

While school gave me a sense of control and purpose, my Jewish identity kept me grounded and helped me cope. Unfortunately, the local Jewish community hadn't made the leap to confront mental health concerns during my childhood years (late 1990s to early 2000s). My mother was a blind spot in my congregation; the leaders and congregants either didn't notice or looked the other way. My synagogue supported my Jewish education by accepting me to religious school on scholarship and raising money to fund my camp retreat trips, so I could feel a sense of belonging and participate with my Jewish peers.

Though I am extremely grateful for the opportunities granted to me by my synagogue, and the financial and emotional support from professionals at Jewish Family & Career Services (JF&CS), I had to create a place for myself in my community. I always had a strong sense of self and personal identity, but I often felt like a burden to the Jewish community at large. I wasn't hearing conversations about mental health, and no one visited my family at home, in the hospitals, or at the rehab centers my mother frequented. I knew I wasn't alone, but I also knew my quiet, internal struggle with anxiety and my mother's problems were invisible and had no place in Jewish communal life.

Then one day when I was fifteen years old, I suddenly experienced an overwhelming sense of comfort and belonging with one simple internet search.

"Why do I pick my skin when I'm anxious?"

Dermatillomania. The word immediately appeared on the screen with a link to someone's blog. It literally means, "manic picking of the skin." In a few short minutes, I learned it's also commonly known as "skin picking disorder," "compulsive skin picking," or "excoriation disorder." People who pick at their skin do so because they have an impaired stress response in the brain. Dermatillomania also is related to trichotillomania (the pulling of one's own hair) and nail biting.

Why do I pick my skin when I'm anxious?

The facts poured in with each search, with each click of my mouse, for hours and hours. For the first time, I no longer felt like a freak with ugly scarred skin. Instead, I felt empowered with new tools, resources, and language to get the help I didn't know I needed. I wasn't alone. Finding out two out of every fifty people live with what I have was so reassuring. I realized the ugliest thing wasn't my skin but the heavy weight of the guilt, resentment, and fear that held me down for so many years.

I was seventeen years old before I was diagnosed with generalized anxiety disorder and body-focused repetitive behavior, also known as BFRB. I started counseling and self-care practices along with antianxiety medication. I still pick my skin and am confronted constantly by friends, family, and co-workers who don't understand I can't just stop. Dermatillomania is always going to be part of me. The work is in fighting the urge to let it take over with its partner anxiety. More important, it is also in forgiving myself when I let the urge take over—and in caring for myself once the damage is done. We're all only human, and I hope my story provides comfort and confidence for others who have their own stories to share. There's power in knowing we can heal together.

- ERIN PIRKLE

PRACTICING 'TIL IT'S PPPERFECT

We took our seats as the bell rang for class to begin. Mr. Harris began passing out the tests, and I immediately felt my heart start to race. That feeling of crippling anxiety took complete hold of me. Sure, high school history wasn't my favorite subject, but I was prepared for this test, and I knew it.

My heart sank when I saw it wasn't multiple choice this time. I wouldn't simply be able to fill in the circles and move on to the next question. Knowing each one would have to be answered in multiple sentences, I began to panic, as I realized how many shapes I would have to perfect as I crafted each letter to complete each answer.

My heart sank as I saw it wasn't multiple choice this time.

I made it through the first few words before I had to write the letter P. I started from the bottom up, first drawing the line and then circling around to form the oval. As I finished drawing, I realized the end of the oval extended past the straight line. Knowing the letter wasn't perfect, I needed to fix it and began to erase and rewrite. I rewrote that letter and had a perfect second P. At that time, however, three was my "lucky" number, so I erased and rewrote it. But the third P wasn't perfect. So, logically to me, I now had to successfully erase and rewrite the letter P nine times (that would be three P's, three times). There was a lot of pressure to get that final ninth P perfect, or else I would have to multiply those nine P's times three and do it again.

I messed up the ninth P. Finally, after erasing and rewriting it twenty-seven times, I was able to move on to the next letter, an A. Twenty-seven more times. The letter after the A was a T, and once again, I had to erase and rewrite that letter twenty-seven times—to complete the cycle of writing three consecutive letters twenty-seven times. As I got to the fourth letter, I knew if I messed it up, I'd have to begin erasing that one, too (thus messing up my pattern of three). I began to really panic, knowing if that should happen, I would have to erase and rewrite the next five letters twenty-seven times each (which would equal erasing and rewriting nine consecutive letters twenty-seven times). Twenty-five minutes had already passed, and I had written only a couple of words in this very long test. I began to shake. As I felt the tears begin to well up, I decided to step outside for a minute.

Two girls stood in front of me at the water fountain. One had a sip of water and began walking away before quickly turning back.

"Let me fill up my water bottle really quick," she said. "I'm so OCD."

As I walked back to the classroom, I knew I couldn't let myself begin to write. I decided I would sit through the test and talk to my teacher afterward. He'd understand.

So I sat there for the rest of the class with pencil in hand, pretending to be engaged in the test. As I sat there, I could feel my mind was about to punish me for not being strong enough to continue with the erasing and rewriting. It told me to count. I counted to eighty. "Again," it said. I counted to eighty again. "Again." "Again." "Again." "Again." By the time the bell rang, I was noticeably in tears and had counted to eighty—fifty-five times.

One of the most difficult things for me back then was realizing I no longer was "normal." And while I cherished my friends and their advice, I couldn't yet bring myself to tell them the truth. While I'm sure they would have comforted me and made me feel better about my situation, I felt being around them was the only place I could still feel normal. I wanted to hold on to that for as long as possible.

By the time the bell rang, I was noticeably in tears and had counted to eighty—fifty-five times.

So each day I'd go to school, plaster a big fake smile on my face and joke around with my friends. That fake smile often would become a real smile, simply because I was smiling. But the feeling that resulted from both the OCD and my inability to talk to those I would most like to confide in left me feeling a nearly unbearable amount of frustration, angst, and anxiety each day after school.

It was during this time when I fell completely in love with music and the piano. Almost every day, as soon as I'd come home, I'd run to the piano and just play for the next three, four, five, six, seven hours. That's where it would all pour out.

While I had to fake normalcy at school, the piano became—and remains to this day—a safe space where I can be myself.

* * *

Recently, I was reminded of the ironic scene at my high school's water fountain while lounging in New York's Washington Square Park.

The piano became—and remains to this day—a safe space where I can be myself.

"Hold on one sec. I need to tie my shoes," I heard a guy yell to his friends, before adding, "I'm so OCD." He tied them in less than five seconds and ran off.

I smiled to myself.

I went home inspired to revisit the journal I kept during high school.

April 2004

It now takes me more than four hours to get in bed. Four hours of fixing, touching, balancing, rearranging, hoarding things next to my bed, hiding all the scissors, perfectly placing my cell phone into the charger many times, turning the lights on and off many times, looking over and over at one picture of my grandparents, looking at the same picture many more times (while blinking), touching every corner in every room, combing my hair excessive times, washing my hands, looking behind every piece of furniture, in every corner in every room many times, smiling into the mirror many times, opening and closing doors, fixing "wrong" steps, and entering and exiting rooms a certain number of times. Sometimes I get into bed after the four hours of compulsions, and I hear my dog in the room adjacent to mine. My mind tells me I have to get up to pet her, or else I don't love her. Of course, I get up and pet her, and then it takes me four more hours to get back in bed.

* * *

I used to get angry when I'd hear someone—after what usually was nothing more than a minor delay—toss it off as having obsessive compulsive disorder.

I didn't realize back then the word OCD most likely became part of these people's vocabularies because of the frequent, casual use of the term on TV and in movies. They almost certainly did not pick up the word from those actually suffering.

Back when I was struggling with a severe form of the disorder, hearing these references made me feel, in a way, possessive of the term, which only made me feel angry.

I sure do wish TV, books, and movies wouldn't throw OCD around so casually. But in the meantime, I'm not bothered by people using the term in the wrong way. Here's why: On nearly every second or third date, there comes a point when the lady I'm out with opens up and tells me her "stuff." Back in high school, when the pretty girls were running around, smiling and casually saying they had OCD, it seemed impossible to me that maybe they were suffering from something too. How wrong I was. Everyone has his or her stuff.

★ ★ ★

Toward the end of those dark days in high school, I reached out to legendary jazz saxophonist Sonny Rollins via his website to tell him how much his music helped me deal with OCD. I was shocked when he responded.

I know it was hard to see during the darkest of days but I am truly thankful for that experience!

"Dear Joe. Your comments were appreciated. We all have to use adversity as an opportunity to find a way. So keep a strong mind throughout this short existence. Your examples give us all hope, as all of us here in this life have to struggle."

Now, quite a few years after cognitive behavior therapy helped put those rough days behind me, I see how right Mr. Rollins was: OCD was nothing more than the greatest opportunity in the world to strengthen my mind and myself.

I know it was hard to see during the darkest of days, but I am truly thankful for that experience and know I would be nowhere near as successful and happy as I am today had it not been for my OCD. People often approach me at my performances and say things like, "You sound like an old man who has been around a while." I'm always incredibly touched by that and totally credit any "feeling" people associate with my music to my experience with OCD.

- JOE ALTERMAN

REPAIRING MY PERSONAL WORLD

I was on the floor again. Rocking back and forth, trying my best to breathe, panicked tears streaming down my face. At that point in my life, anxiety attacks were a routine part of my day, as if I had a Google calendar event on my schedule:

Get up for class: 8:30 a.m.
Finish writing a paper: 11:00 a.m.
Go to work: 3:00 p.m.
Anxiety attack: 10:00 p.m.

It's hard to describe how those moments felt. Seconds seemed like hours; minutes seemed like days; hours seemed like years. Most frightening was the feeling of being alone—a nasty, monstrous, all-enveloping cloud of isolation and worthlessness. It became increasingly difficult to believe others around me had their own hardships. Everyone I passed on the street seemed all put together. There was no way there were others like me. I was obviously just weak.

I never considered that repairing the world starts with repairing myself.

At my Jewish high school, I remember learning about *tikkun olam* and the concept of repairing the world. But I felt so helpless to the task of making the world a better place. If I could barely handle my own issues, how could I help others? I never considered that repairing the world starts with repairing myself.

My understanding of mental health as a child was limited. It was always an extremely guarded subject in my community as I was growing up. The only information about mental illness and treatment I received came largely from pop culture. I knew, for example, Frasier Crane from Cheers was a psychiatrist. Fictional characters who existed in sitcom worlds went to therapy, but it didn't seem like people in real life did.

"Therapy" was a word whispered among gossipers, not something that was spoken about openly in my community. When I was about twelve years old, someone I knew offhandedly mentioned attending therapy regularly, and I was shocked. Everything seemed so "normal," I couldn't wrap my head around it. Rather than seeing therapy as a road to progress, I saw it as an indication there was something wrong with that person.

Eventually, I found a Jewish community that taught me the importance of taking care of oneself and of shedding the stigma around therapy and mental health treatment. It was this community that quite literally saved my life in college.

I attended a huge state school in the south, so inevitably, the Jewish students banded together. We created a safe space for each other in our Hillel building. This space became home to me. There was seldom a day you wouldn't find me there, just existing in a place where I felt peace. The people there became my social network, my best friends, my lifeline. I had never been in a place where everybody was so open and encouraged to speak up about their hardships. After an intense exam, we were each other's decompressors. And after the Pittsburgh synagogue shooting in 2018, we were each other's shoulders to cry on.

In that space, we existed for each other, yet it still took some time for me to appreciate just how much I needed their support.

During my last semester, I reached my breaking point. Despite the community I found at Hillel, I felt myself slipping away, as if the real Elana was fading from existence. After days of walking up to her office and turning away right before walking in, I finally gathered the courage to speak to my Hillel director about it. When I sat down opposite her, the floodgates opened. I told her everything: I wasn't sleeping, I was binge eating, my body was constantly aching, I hadn't felt happy in a long time. With each word I spoke, I became more scared. Terrible thoughts erupted in my head: *She's going to think I'm insane, that I can't handle things on my own. She's going to be scared of me, or upset that I'm weak.*

I will never forget her response.

"You aren't broken. You're whole, and you just need help to feel that way."

This concept was radical to me. And so deeply Jewish: to intrinsically value your life. It is the heartbeat of our people—to realize we are all created *b'tzelem elohim* (in God's image).

"You aren't broken. You're whole, and you just need help to feel that way."

To paraphrase the Talmud, whoever saves a single life, it is as if he or she saved an entire world. I always used to view this saying in an outward sense, but I have come to realize it is just as poignant as an inward-facing prescription. Once you understand the woman next to you was born with divine value, you have to realize you were as well. You are that single life worth saving, just as much as the next person. And if you have the chance and the support to save yourself, you have saved an entire world.

I've carried this notion with me ever since. My Hillel director helped me find the courage to go to my first therapy session, and I continue to go regularly. After graduating, I got a job across the country at a Jewish nonprofit in Salt Lake City, despite being afraid of the distance from my comfort zone—not to mention my built-in support network back home. But that's the beautiful thing about a Jewish community: It waits for you everywhere, ready to be there for you, ready to stand by you. The decision to work in a Jewish nonprofit came easily to me.

As I have started to repair my personal world, my body, and my spirit, things have started to fall into place. I came to see that because I was able to make a space to help myself, I am so lucky to be in a position where I can help others. I now work with Jewish college students who are in the same position I was in just months ago—trying to figure out what their passions are, who their real friends are, and, most important, who they want to become. I just want them to know what they already are. I want them to see themselves as whole and worthy. People need to understand this truth: Every life is one worth saving.

- ELANA ANN FAUTH

An earlier version of this story first appeared on heyalma.com, an online community for Jewish women from 70 Faces Media.

NOBODY SAID LIFE WAS FAIR...
SOMETIMES YOU NEED TO MAKE A BIG CHANGE

I was the one who always thought people were crazy for breathing into a paper bag...until it was me.

On April 20, 2015, I received a call that would turn my world upside down. It wasn't the type of call one might expect to warrant such a dramatic feeling; nor, at the time, did I realize how life changing it would be. That call ended up affecting the next several weeks, months, and years more than I ever could have imagined.

My wife was entering her eighth month of pregnancy, while I was battling a public relations storm at work that included countless death threats against me and those I care about. As a Jew, I was being sent graphic emails and images calling for a second Holocaust. Some people threatened to protest my home, my work, and other areas that would affect many people. Others threatened to harm my family.

Until this point, I had never been an emotional person. I was the type who kept my feelings bottled up, because I never wanted to feel like I was burdening someone with my issues. I needed to be the person to keep those around me safe, motivated, and focused. This case was no different. I needed to be the glue to keep our team from being torn apart by accusations that later would be found to be mostly false and largely mischaracterized. I did the best job I could holding it together—until it all started to fall apart on April 27.

I was home alone, trying to turn the television on so I could watch an interview a reporter was doing about this issue, when I finally broke. I found myself throwing the remote control across the room and crying hysterically on my couch. I called my wife, who could hear the fear and anxiety in my voice. She came home immediately, only to find me sitting with a paper bag in my hand. I can't remember if breathing into that bag worked. It was all a blur. I eventually got passed that moment, because I had to. We were about to welcome our daughter into the world. I was embarrassed. I felt like I had lost control of my life.

Several months later, I was sitting in my living room angry about a phone conversation I just had, and everything felt like it was resurfacing. I could feel my blood boiling. I was shaking. I don't know how or why this next episode occurred, but I found myself looking for the phone I had thrown at a wall across the room. My wife came downstairs to see what had happened, and I couldn't even speak. It was like I blacked out with my eyes open. I was shaking, scared, anxious. I felt completely lost. I didn't see a need for tomorrow. That was my true breaking point and a sign I couldn't get through this alone. I needed help.

I started to ask around for suggestions for therapists. What really shocked me was that everyone I asked had a recommendation, because they all had seen one. It immediately made me realize this feeling of helplessness wasn't as "weird" or "unusual" as I had convinced myself it was. I began seeing someone and taking medication to help with my depression and anxiety that fall.

 **I needed help.**

The initial therapy sessions weren't great. In fact, I found the therapist to be relatively uninterested, robotic, and disengaged in what I had to say. But he gave me medicine—medicine that eventually would make me feel human again. Although it didn't start that way.

To get me back to a better place, I am pretty sure this therapist prescribed too much medicine. I felt numb, overly stoic, and indifferent to anything and everything that came my way. I was calm—too calm. While I wasn't feeling the same anger and sadness I once was, I am not sure I felt happy. I just felt "blah." But I was hesitant to make any changes, because those terribly bad feelings were gone.

Not too long after that, my wife, our daughter, and I moved to a new city, and I began working remotely in the same position I had been in. I began seeing a new therapist, and I will never forget what she said after I described what I had been going through. She looked me right in the eyes and told me things would never change while I remained in my job. I thought that was ridiculous! There was no way I was leaving a job I loved with people who supported me, had my back, were good to me, and taught me many valuable life lessons. So, I found another way to stay happy—or, at least, what I thought was happy.

Over the course of my adulthood, I would start and stop exercising more often than I care to admit. We moved to a new neighborhood that had an Orange Theory Fitness studio, and I thought I would check it out, mostly because my wife had joined and told me I should.

March 19, 2017, would prove to be the first day of the rest of my life. I found happiness in the method of exercise that OTF offers its members. I found enjoyment in sweating out my stress. I felt motivated by the coaches to become a better version of myself. Shortly after I joined, I began supplementing those workouts with personal training sessions. Exercise turned out to be part of the answer I had been looking for. I emphasize the word "part."

While I began to feel better, mentally and physically, I never could get out of my mind what my new therapist said in our first meeting. Was it possible that I could never find balance or sanity in the job I was in? I had felt so happy there for so long. Surely this instance two years earlier was an exception and not the rule. I knew how to do my job. I was pretty good at it. I had autonomy with the right balance of support. I loved most of the people I interacted with. They were my family, and I couldn't imagine leaving them.

And then one day, the phone rang. Sometimes opportunity knocks, and you don't answer the door. This time I did, and it was someone from an organization I did not know well. She said all the right things, focused on all the right areas, and offered me the chance to see if a new beginning was really what I needed. I had been offered these opportunities before but never thought twice about them. This time, I took the leap (and the advice from the therapist) and decided to leave my home away from home. I had been thinking about what my therapist said regarding what needed to change, thinking about new challenges I may need, and also reflecting on everything I had missed out in my family from the travel associated with my job.

I knew I was making the right move toward happiness, but I was reluctant to give up the meds I had depended on for three years. They made me feel like I had control over my life. They made my wife happier, because I was happier. They let me enjoy the precious moments with my daughter. I desperately wanted to let them go but was terrified of how I might feel if I did. Until I tried.

My therapist was impressed with my progress and wanted to lower the dose of the medicine targeting my depression. We lowered it, and it worked. We lowered it again, and it worked again. She then recommended we lower the medicine treating my anxiety, so we did, and it worked. I began using it only on an "as-needed" basis. Then we removed the antidepressants and the antianxiety medicine completely.

Everyone's journey is different, and this feels like the right path for me.

So, here I am trying to navigate happiness in a new way, in a new city, in a new job, with a new lust for life. I already have encountered some hiccups through the realization that, in some ways, life was easier on the meds. Everyone's journey is different, and this feels like the right path for me.

If I had to summarize this experience into bullet points, it would look like this:

- It's okay to feel defeated. Everyone does at some point.
- Help won't seek you out. You must find it and embrace it.
- Let the baggage go. It's okay to acknowledge you've got issues. We all do.
- Be open to possibilities that take you off the path you thought you were supposed to be on.
- Be open to finding happiness in places you weren't expecting.
- Let others in.
- Look for ways to be better, and remember perfection isn't attainable by anyone.

The future can be only as bright as we choose it to be.

- A MAN WITH AN OPEN MIND

LESSONS LEARNED FROM MY PARENTS

When I think about my dad at home through all the years of my growing up, I think of him as alone. And when I think about my mom through those same years, I think of her as lonely.

My dad, who was living with bipolar disorder, spent months at a time inside our house, often in his bed, almost always alone. My mom would go to work every day, and my brother and I would go to school. When we got home, there he would be, on the couch, watching television.

I was a kid. It never occurred to me to wonder about how alone he was. He was my dad—funny, smart, devoted to his family. Most of the time, he was also bitter, angry, and dark. Then would come the weeks of mania, when he was full of ideas, excitement, and risky behavior. I remember driving in the car with him as a little girl, believing his talk of empires to be built and incredible ideas to be implemented.

 **She held him and us together.**

In the 1950s and 1960s, no one understood my father's mood swings. My parents' friends wondered, and perhaps pitied, but mostly they stayed away. My dad's parents fretted that they had done something wrong to cause such brokenness. My mother's parents urged her to leave my dad and bring my brother and me to live in their house. Instead, my mother stood by my father, the love of her life. She held him and us together. There were no support groups for her; synagogue was not a safe place; and her friends were not equipped to understand. I wonder who possibly could have listened to her without judgment, even if she could have articulated her sorrow and her rage. She must have been very lonely.

Mom was strong and stoic. She would come home from a full day of work at her father's pharmacy on a Sunday to find my dad, my brother, and me all camped out in front of the television, all of us still in pajamas at six o'clock. No chores on our short list would have been accomplished, no dinner prepared. We had eaten bowls of Wheaties for breakfast and Ritz crackers with peanut butter for lunch. Did she seethe inside? As a kid, it never seemed that way to me. She just seemed glad to see us all.

I would help her set the table, and we would eat warmed frozen dinners or cans of Dinty Moore stew. We ate a lot of pizza, McDonalds, and submarine sandwiches. Sitting together at the table was more important to her than what we ate.

"Some people have a sickness in their stomachs or their lungs. I have a sickness in my head."

Conversation at those dinners was freewheeling and wonderful. I remember current events, Dad's telling jokes, and lots of sports talk. There was also open talk about the upside-down nature of our family life. Everyone else's daddy got up every morning and went to work. I am sure I complained about coming home on school days for lunch to my dad instead of my mom. I am certain I asked why he couldn't just go to work.

I can hear my father say, "Some people have a sickness in their stomachs or their lungs. I have a sickness in my head." I believe he said, "A voice in my head tells me all the things I cannot do." And yet, he was my dad.

I was nine years old when Dad was diagnosed. I have my journal from 1968, and in my block print, very large across the page, I wrote: "Daddy has manic depression." I must have felt relieved this thing had a name.

All of those conversations taught me to look for the strength in people. My mother taught us the illness did not define my father. In her estimation, he was brilliant and funny with a disorder that kept him from fulfilling his potential. I grew up to be stronger because of my father's illness.

But I also grew up fearful about my own mental health. I was an over-achiever, often suffering stomach aches as I pushed myself always to be as perfect as I could be. I did not want to give my mother one more reason to worry. I did not want to be bipolar. It took me years into adulthood before I learned I could slow down and stop running from a mental illness that has not affected me after all.

But I also grew up fearful about my own mental health.

From the beginning of my rabbinate, I have dedicated myself to creating a safe space and removing the stigma of mental illness for congregational families. My parents gave me the gift of feeling free to ask questions and to receive the best answers they could give. It was not an easy childhood, but their wise coping meant I learned lessons for life.

I have always spoken in sermons about mental illness, sharing my father's story as well as my own after I experienced a year and a half of anxiety and depression. I wrote about it and taught about it. The more I made myself vulnerable, the more I was able to help. Congregants who struggle seek me out, and others ask if I will speak with their family members, friends, and neighbors. I meet with whoever seeks a listening ear and open heart. I make recommendations of professionals and programs from a list of referrals I have built carefully over almost twenty years on the pulpit. I believe most rabbis want to help. Someone seeking understanding will know immediately if a rabbi is able to follow through on his or her desire.

Today more than ever, Jewish congregations are open to facing mental health issues in a straight-forward, inclusive way. There is no one unaffected by mental illness him or herself, in one's family, or among one's circle of friends. Along a continuum and across a lifetime, we humans all find our places in terms of our mental wellness and vulnerability.

I think a great deal about my parents every May as my synagogue honors Mental Health Awareness Month. We educate, hold panels, celebrate a special Shabbat, teach tools for resiliency and mental health, and post to our blog. This past May, we walked in silent meditation from our daily chapel to the bima in the sanctuary to receive Torah, a powerful reenactment of Mount Sinai, where everyone received Torah in his or her own way. God does not see anyone as broken; everyone is created in God's image. We walked together as a community, from the four-year-old twins skipping along to the ninety-year-old couple walking carefully with canes. Being together in a community where everyone is accepted as "just fine," just the way they are, is a most powerful sustainer of mental wellness. Everyone who was in synagogue on that Shabbat felt this crucial teaching in our very souls.

But what about everyone who was not able to be in synagogue with us? What about those who struggle with mental illness in their homes or in facilities and cannot leave, trapped there, unable to enter into our community of faith? What about the caregivers of those people, too exhausted and fearful of stigma to come out and join us in community? They probably do not see a sanctuary; rather, they see an unbearable barrier to entry. How can we begin to change this reality for Jewish people who feel isolated due to mental illness?

If you are struggling with mental health issues and you feel alone, reach out to your rabbi, your local Jewish Family Services organization, or one of the mental health agencies in your area. Reach out in any way you feel able, so someone who cares can meet you halfway. Even if you can only reach out a very short distance, I hope an empathic, caring person will meet you the rest of the way.

If you are lonely because you are a caregiver to someone struggling with mental health issues, I hope you find a friend, family member, or professional to listen, share, and allow you to strengthen yourself.

We must continue to speak out. We must work hard to enable people to feel safe enough to be vulnerable in our sanctuary spaces. Our tasks are to open our hearts, educate ourselves toward deep understanding, and become empowered advocates.

We must continue to speak out.

This is the work that remains to be done. This is the work I am called to do in memory of my parents—a brilliant, mentally ill father and a steadfast, loyal mother. This is the life-saving work I commit myself to doing, not just in the month of May, but always.

- RABBI PAULA MACK-DRILL

MY EMOTIONAL ROLLERCOASTER

My story starts at the end of freshman year at Emory University. After going home for summer break, I fell into a pretty substantial depression. At the time, I didn't realize I was depressed. I knew something was off—I felt disconnected, lonely, out of sync—but didn't understand the symptoms. Thinking it would go away, I didn't tell a soul. Looking back, it was silly not to tell my parents; they are nurturing and intelligent doctors.

My depression continued for a few weeks into fall semester, but then I started to feel better. I was very social and had a lot of friends, which helped me get back to a better day-to-day mood. I was really coming into my own and enjoying the good life of a "fratty," fun, loving person. I was living in a fraternity house, enjoying the (probably too) social atmosphere, and smoking a lot of weed. I had a pretty crazy, party-filled year and actually got mono. Despite my poor physical health, I felt like I was in a stable mental space. I also dropped pre-med during that time, and for the spring semester I looked to improve my academics and thrive.

But about six weeks in, I started acting very strangely. I have always been a very goofy, outgoing, social person, but some of the things I was saying were just absurd. I announced to my friends and even some professors I was "purely enlightened," I had "reached nirvana," I was a "prophet." Little did I know at the time, I was having a manic episode. I felt intense happiness and excitement, but these feelings were stemming from an unnatural source (the imbalance of chemicals in my brain). Typically, this much energy is followed by a crash, and sure enough, I spiraled into depression. This rapid instability often plagues those with bipolar disorder.

I needed medical attention, and I'm thankful one of my professors notified the school's student health center. In the next few days, I met with a caseworker who set me up with a school psychiatrist who helped me discuss the situation with my parents. She prescribed an antipsychotic medicine, which led to an eventual "come-down." After several weeks of intense highs, I experienced a terrorizing crash. I felt deeply depressed.

Unable to study or take tests, I came home before spring break to recuperate and planned to return to school as fast as I could. Unfortunately, I wasn't stabilized in such a short time and decided to spend the rest of spring semester at home in Florida, where my parents connected me with a therapist and psychiatrist. I'm lucky my entire family supported me from the beginning of this arduous time.

The next two months took me on an emotional rollercoaster. For about two weeks, I felt great—like I was beginning to understand the ways in which you can transform suffering into deep peace. I began reading *The Power of Now*, which eventually would shape my entire spiritual foundation and transform my daily existence. But that peace was short lasting. My depression worsened significantly, and I even lost the desire to read the book.

Shortly before leaving school, I had begun a relationship with a girl and fallen in love very quickly. We continued to speak frequently while I was home, but it was hard for her to feel the same way about me after being together for not even three weeks. I hoped she would develop those feelings over time, but it really wasn't a healthy relationship. At a certain point, she was a crutch for me. I was using my desire for us to be together as a qualification for healthier days.

The next two months took me on an emotional rollercoaste

She ended things a few months after I got home, saying she just wanted to be friends. Blinded by love, I imagined we'd have a great friendship, and when I was better, we'd simply pick up where we left off. The idea that she actually did end things hit me like a truck about a week later. I felt a sickening, rotting darkness at my core. I almost threw up. This darkness was heavier and more serious than anything I had ever experienced, as I now was feeling loss and utter heartbreak as well. I'm an emotional person. I give myself to people fully and love very deeply. This pain shattered me. I felt cut off from the personal self I once identified with. In my mind, I no longer was the fun-loving Jacob everyone knew and adored. Now, without my presumed 'soul-mate,' I felt like I was absolutely nothing.

I can describe the next three months as a downward spiral of emotions. But it's hard to explain the extent of the despair, hopelessness, sadness, and loneliness I felt.

FINALLY, at the end of three months of my most intense depression, something miraculous happened. I'll never forget the day. After a morning of my typical mental barrage of negative thoughts, I was exercising on the elliptical machine and watching the movie *Ray* on TV. At the end of the workout, I started to feel something clear up, and I texted my friend Jasmine. Like a madman, I started venting my heart out, just outpouring emotions of my experience and how tough the past five months had been. Since the heartbreak, I rarely talked to anyone in person or through text. This was tough, because I am a very social person. Depression really isolates you. But something in me shifted that day. Maybe it was the medicine I was taking. Maybe I began healing from the heartbreak. Maybe I needed to hit rock bottom, before I could really rise from the ashes. The quote "sometimes you have to be at your lowest point before you are most ready for change" is very fitting. Whatever it was, I felt an unending sense of gratitude, as I had a new chance to live a bright life filled with joy, love, and peace.

Like a madman, I started venting my heart out, just outpouring emotions of my experience...

For the first time in a very long while, I felt mental clarity. The weight of the world was off my shoulders, and there was a deep instinct inside me to continue my spiritual journey. My first step was to reread *The Power of Now*. Its words rang with truth and resonated fiercely within my heart. I had lost track of so much during my college experience, but now I felt I was learning to identify with my deepest essence. I realized that during my depressive episode, I identified too strongly with the toxic thoughts in my head. Now I was beginning to feel in tune with the underlying source of existence. With a fresh start, I could learn to transcend any mental chatter with mindfulness and meditation. I realized my thoughts were constantly wandering to the past or future, when there truly is only the present moment—the Now.

I was diagnosed officially with bipolar disorder.

At this point it was July, and to return to Emory in the fall, I would need medical clearance a month before the semester. Unfortunately, I missed the deadline. This ended up being a great blessing, though, as I could use the extended period to learn to live a fuller life one day at a time. I had five months before I could go back to school in the spring—time I used to read books about Buddhism, Hinduism, religion, spirituality, meditation, mindfulness, and more. I developed a meditation practice, which helped deepen the inner peace I felt. When I returned to school, I became an interdisciplinary studies major, where you pick a topic and then approach it from different disciplines. I focused on how individuals share holistic wellness techniques like meditation and mindfulness via technology.

That semester, I was diagnosed officially with bipolar disorder. I had been experiencing fatigue and exhaustion from time to time, but even during depressive and hypomanic (not quite fully manic) cycles, my overall health, mood, energy, and happiness levels were much more consistent. I became more effective at managing school and extracurricular activities, many of which focused on helping individuals going through similar struggles learn how to transform their experience into peace, joy, and liberation.

I graduated in May 2018, and while I have come a long way, I continue to have ups and downs. I'm very open about my experiences with bipolar disorder. Moving away from a career in medicine but toward one in overall health, I am a life coach helping people on their spiritual and wellness journeys incorporate meditation and mindfulness into their lives. In addition to working one-on-one with clients, I have spoken to a variety of audiences at companies like Coca Cola and Delta as well as at Emory.

My conscious perception of the world changes often because of my mood, but it gives me strength and the skills to find balance. When I have a depressive episode, I know it's temporary, and I have worked to find meaning after each one. My instability has almost been my superpower. It has forced me to master balance.

- JACOB AQUA

HIS SECRETS

I'm a thirty-nine-year-old mother of two in suburban Atlanta. Ethan and Layla are the most incredible little people in the universe. I am surrounded by wonderful and generous family and friends, and I love my job.

Sounds pretty great, right? It's a beautiful picture. And it's true. I'm pretty lucky. But it's not that easy nor that perfect. There's something really big missing from my life.

A few years ago, my husband, Adam, committed suicide. It's really hard. It's hard to know. It's hard to say. I'm sure it's really hard to hear.

I think people wouldn't be as uncomfortable if he died another way. I think it would be less difficult to say my husband died of cancer or a heart attack. People hate physical diseases, but they understand them—a tumor, a blockage, or something awful medicine just couldn't undo. No one says, "A stroke? Why couldn't he just shake it off?" But with suicide, it's an uncomfortable silence. The unspoken judgement. The questions: What happened? Was it sudden? Did he suffer from depression? Anxiety? Did you know? Were you surprised? And I'm OK with the questions. But it gives me pause. If people are uncomfortable with the cause of his death, imagine how hard it would have been for them to understand how he was feeling when he was still alive.

We met in college. He knew right away we were meant to be together, even if it took me a couple of years to figure it out. He was so much fun to be around. He was spontaneous and funny. He knew everyone and remembered details from everyone's stories. He was fiercely loyal to his family and his friends—the kind of person you could call at two o'clock in the morning. He would leap out of bed and rush to your side, not only with support but with a toolbox, a cell phone, and seventy-five possible solutions to whatever you were facing. He loved entertaining, cooking on his Big Green Egg, and drinking fine wine and spirits. He lived for his vacations—his escape from the "real world" to relax at the beach and spend time with family and close friends.

The outside world didn't know Adam suffered from severe depression and anxiety. We had been married for several years before I even knew. Sure, sometimes he was a little defensive. He complained he wasn't able to sleep. I could see he was very stressed out and had a hard time recovering from certain situations. "Tell me what's going on," I'd say. "I'm fine," he'd reply, and change the subject. "Do you think you should talk to someone?" "ABSOLUTELY NOT! I don't even want to talk to you about it. Can we change the subject?"

The outside world didn't know Adam suffered from severe depression and anxiety.

Adam seemed to be a rock, able to deal with it all. We suffered through infertility, two miscarriages, job stresses, and moving to Alabama with few friends nearby. He got me through all of it. Then there was one time about eight years ago. Ethan was probably a year old. I had to go out of town for a weekend, and I left him home with Adam. When I returned, Adam told me he had a bad day, and if Ethan hadn't been there, if he had been home alone, he wouldn't have made it through the night. It was then, when he almost took his life the first time, that I truly learned about his depression. It was only then that he started to seek help.

He went to several doctors. He didn't want to talk; he just wanted medication to make him feel better. He got some sleeping pills and some antianxiety medication, and he seemed to be a little happier, a little less short-fused, a little more involved and interested in Ethan's and my life. I was sworn to secrecy. No one was allowed to know Adam suffered from mental illness and took medicine for it. It would make him look weak, keep him from progressing in his work. Our family and friends would judge him and think he wasn't good enough. I didn't really know anything about mental illness. Adam did. All those nights he didn't sleep, he read and learned. So I listened to him and kept my promise.

We moved back to Atlanta, and it was a roller coaster for him. He had a new job where he wasn't treated well. He changed jobs but still didn't find his niche. Adam was a dedicated worker and supremely good at what he did. His employees called on him to be a mentor, and he was his boss' "right-hand man." But he wasn't happy. He would tell me about other opportunities he learned about. Once I told him, "I just wish you could find something that makes you happy. You never seem happy. I don't care what you make, I don't care where we live, just do what makes you happy." He was so upset. I thought I was being supportive, but I had blown his cover. "What do you mean I don't seem happy? What do I do that makes me seem unhappy?"

He still saw his psychiatrist in Alabama about every six months. He would tell the doctor everything was great, and the medication would be refilled. And he would come back home, tell me he was fine, and disappear into our room to watch TV alone.

We went through life, as everyone does, with ups and downs. Job losses, family situations. Amazing vacations. New jobs.

We went through a time when everything was great. We both had new jobs. We had bought a new house. Ethan was starting kindergarten. What a high! To be exactly where you want to be, with the people you want to be with.

But like all good things, it slowly came to an end. Adam's work got more stressful. I became pregnant with our daughter and had various pregnancy complications. And he started to withdraw. He would get home from work and not want to talk. He told me it was because he had been entertaining customers all day. He would disappear into our room to watch TV. He would ask not to attend various plans we had. He wasn't sleeping well again, and the medicine wasn't helping. But he didn't want more, and he did NOT want to go back to the doctor any time soon. He insisted he didn't need more help, and he refused to talk to anyone. And no one could know. Our friends would judge him. He wouldn't get that promotion he was vying for. By this time, I was also a mom of two with a full-time job. I was tired, short-fused, angry, and nervous about how things were going to be. I felt like I had the weight of the world on my shoulders. One time I suggested we go to therapy. I didn't think I was coping well. He got really mad. "You're fine. Nothing is wrong with you. You aren't the one who has anxiety." It was hard. I felt all alone. I knew I couldn't continue to overlook my stress and occasional sadness and take a backseat to him. But I knew I couldn't load more onto his plate.

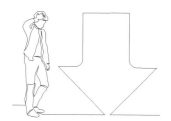

No one was allowed to know Adam suffered from mental illness...

Then, in October 2016, he lost his job. I offered to come home. He told me he needed to be alone. And like I had done so many times, I respected his wishes. I gave him his space. And in that time, he went out and purchased a gun.

He made me dinner that night. He was upset and couldn't look me in the eye. I didn't know what to say to him either, as I was tired, sad, scared. Scared for him going through the awful process of looking for a new job. Wondering how I was going to help him fill his time without drowning in his depression. Worrying whether we were going to be able to keep the house, keep the kids in daycare, literally how we were going to make it through. By the way, I was NOT to tell anyone he had lost his job.

He told me he was in bad shape. He said he made an appointment with his doctor the next morning. He had to leave for Alabama really early to arrive right when the office opened. He took a shower, got dressed, wore a nice shirt. He took Ethan to the bus stop and left for "his doctor." I offered to go with him, but he said no. He needed to be alone.

I never saw him again.

At Adam's funeral and the months that followed, people expressed their shock. The things some would say! "Adam seemed so strong." "He saved my life a few years ago. Let me tell you what he did." "I looked up to him so much." "Jenn, why didn't you tell me?" The worst I heard was "Adam was a coward. How dare he do that to you?"

I still say Adam was the strongest person I will ever meet. He once told me he had suicidal thoughts since he was sixteen years old. Despite being surrounded by family and friends, he suffered alone and in silence for twenty years before he lost his battle. He was a warrior who loved me like no one else ever will. Who idolized his children. And he fought all the sadness, hopelessness, and despair for a long time, so he could be with us and be there for us. But the disease won.

You are probably thinking, "Why did you let him walk out the door if he was so upset? Why didn't you tell anyone he was so sick? Why didn't you insist he get help?" I bet you wonder what it was really like. And how you would have done it differently. I relive over and over that twenty-four hours—in fact the whole year—that led up to that horrible day. I wish I had said this or hadn't said that. I wish I hadn't let him walk out the door. I wish. I wish. I wish. I wish I could have changed my story and saved his life one more time.

I often Monday-morning quarterback the last year of his life. There were a lot of signs. I didn't know. I did the best I could with what I had, and I have to accept that. I can't change the past. But I can affect the future. I can tell you what I know now. I can help you and your loved ones recognize signs: withdrawal, anger, sleeplessness, hopelessness, mood swings, a strong desire to keep up the appearance of being great.

The biggest thing is keeping secrets. I don't mean little things. I'm talking about things that shouldn't be kept a secret. Major life events, good and bad. I can't tell you how many times I was "not allowed" to tell people about things. Then, he would bring them up at a dinner party. People would say, "Jenn, I can't believe you didn't tell me that." I lost friends over keeping secrets. But, of course, my marriage was more important than those people, so I justified it. Secrets are exhausting.

Some people have opened up to me over the past two years. Their spouse had a problem with depression, and they weren't able to talk to anyone about it, because they had promised to keep a secret. So they both suffered alone. That was my exact situation. But I wasn't alone, and neither are you.

So, why do I tell my sad story? Because I want to scream from the top of my lungs that if you suffer from anxiety, depression, or any other mental health issue, don't keep it a secret! It is NOT something to be ashamed of. It is NOT a weakness. It is a disease. You can ask for help. You can find someone to talk to. You are important.

Tell that to yourself. Tell that to your spouse. Your children. Your friends. Everyone you meet. Don't make negative comments about mental health. Support initiatives that increase mental health coverage with insurance companies. Suicide is not a punchline in a joke. Depression and anxiety aren't something to avoid just because they aren't pretty. Be kind to everyone. Even the happiest person you know might be suffering privately.

Let people help you. If you know others who suffer from this disease, be there for them. Understand this is a problem with the chemicals in their brain, so don't tell them to "get over it." Think about the silent messages you might be sending. More important, seek help. If you can't convince someone else to get help, raise your hand, and get help for yourself.

I can't bring Adam back. I can't give my kids their father. I can't change my story. But maybe I can change your story. And maybe by encouraging those who need help to get it, others will have the strength to get through another day. And another day after that.

- JENNIFER GREENBERG

LESSONS FROM LOSS

I am the youngest of four boys, with a thirteen-year gap between my oldest brother, Gabriel, and me. We grew up in a close-knit family with our dad, who was a rabbi, and our mom, a wonderful homemaker and courtroom stenographer.

In 1973, my father took a rabbinic position in the small borough of Pottstown, Pennsylvania. Gabriel, who had just turned thirteen and was academically gifted, had no interest in changing schools again and going to the public high school in such a rural community. He asked my parents if he could go away to an all-boys yeshiva to study. I think he wanted not only to get away from rural life but to ground himself in a school where he could excel in Judaic studies and stay put for four years, regardless of where my dad went professionally. Gabe was always very smart and practical. So in the fall of 1974, he packed his bags and headed off to the Talmudic Academy, outside Baltimore, to begin eighth grade.

 **In many ways, that was the last time we saw Gabriel.**

My parents were happy Gabe was eager to get a Jewish education. They understood his desire to stay grounded somewhere, although they were not so happy about sending their child away to school. But then they met and quickly befriended Rabbi Shapiro, the guidance counselor and "point person," who promised to look after Gabe. He assured my parents Gabe would call weekly and write often, and if, God forbid, there were ever a problem, they were only two hours away by car. All would be fine.

They hugged and kissed, and said goodbye and drove off with my other brothers, Elliott and Larry, and me in the car seat waving goodbye.

In many ways, that was the last time we saw Gabriel. I mean, we saw him again, but he was never the same.

My parents would speak to Gabe regularly, but my mother recalled that after a few months he seemed distant, and she sensed something was wrong. She called Rabbi Shapiro and asked that he check in with Gabe and make sure he was adjusting well. He assured her he would. My mother was so indebted to Rabbi Shapiro that she needle-pointed him a pillow—a small token for looking after the welfare of their first born.

When Gabriel came home to visit, he was a different person—not because he was going through puberty, but different in spirit. Disturbed. Angry. Inappropriate. He would erupt into terrible tantrums like a three-year-old. He would become violent. He was quick to cry and would push away from an embrace or any physical affection.

This was not the same boy who was dropped off a few months earlier.

After the second semester began, Gabriel begged not to return for the following year. I was too young to remember, but my parents recall the look in his eyes as he pleaded not to return. In hindsight, it was the cry of an innocent man being forced to go to prison. What was it all about?

My parents quickly agreed, and Gabe did not return to the yeshiva. But his behavior stayed with him. He was still disturbed, angry, and inappropriate. We all could only wonder, why did he change? What happened to my brother, my parents' first-born son?

As I grew up and got to know Gabe, I guess it was fair to say he was different. Not in appearance or dress, but different in behavior. He marched to his own rhythm and had his own style. He would laugh at his own jokes, and do or say wild or outlandish things to get a reaction from people. Somehow, he just knew what your "buttons" were, and he loved to push them to evoke a response at all costs. If something happened Gabe did not like, he would get angry and loud, and lash out with hurtful, mean things. Occasionally, he would get violent. Throughout it all, Gabe maintained his scholastic abilities. He was a genius. He could skip a class for six weeks straight and still ace the final. The problem was, he had no drive. He would start school and then drop out. My parents stayed firm: "If you are not in college, then we will not provide you with room and board." So at nineteen, he ventured out into the real world and saw it was full of challenges and pitfalls. Before long he was back at home and back in school. And then the cycle would start again. He would drop out and be kicked out of the house.

When anyone in our family was around Gabe, we walked on eggshells. He was a tinderbox waiting to explode.

After many years, Gabe seemed to find his rhythm. When he was about twenty-five, he joined the air force; graduated college (with honors, of course); met a girl and got married; and then signed up for rabbinical school. He was still odd and quirky, but if there was one profession that welcomed odd and quirky, it was the rabbinate. He earned ordination, got a job, and had a beautiful baby girl. Things were moving in the right direction for Gabe, and we were all happy for him.

Then suddenly, everything spiraled out of control. He could not handle his job, and his marriage was on the rocks.

 **He was a tinderbox waiting to explode.**

I got the call on July 17, 1996, when I was traveling in Israel. I'll never forget my mother's words: "David, you have to come home. Gabriel committed suicide."

From that moment on, we were a changed family. First, we started never taking anything for granted. We started making sure to end every phone call and every e-mail with "I love you." We began to hug often. And we started to talk a lot. Now, I speak with each of my brothers about once a day, and during football season, we speak hourly.

The other significant thing that changed was we began to better understand Gabe and to unpack whatever baggage he had had. We were almost like investigators researching medications, therapies, and behaviors to complete the complicated puzzle of our brother. There were many confidentiality issues that could not be circumvented, but in the end, I figured out there was an event or a series of events that severely traumatized Gabe when he was younger. Yet while the puzzle was coming together, there was one giant piece in the middle still missing.

In March 2007, we found that missing piece. We learned Ephraim Shapiro, the guidance counselor and so-called "rabbi" at the Talmudic Academy in Baltimore–the very man who had promised to "look after my parents' little boy" and the one my mother needle-pointed a pillow for–had sexually molested and raped hundreds of boys during the years Gabe was a student there. After what had happened became clear, survivors of Shapiro confirmed the series of traumatic and life-altering events my brother had endured.

Not a day goes by when I don't think of him or when I am not filled with regret. It is sadly ironic that I learned much more about my brother and the differences and challenges he had in his life AFTER he died.

Today, like Gabe, I am a congregational rabbi. In that role, I have a unique peephole into people's families and lives, which enables me to claim with certainty that almost every family has someone who is suffering from a mental health challenge. These illnesses do not discriminate between religion, color, sex, or race. Depression is the most notable, but I have seen my share of paranoia, obsessive compulsive disorder (OCD), anxiety, and bipolar disorder; all are rampant in communities like ours. The difference between these and, say, cancer is that we still seem to whisper when someone is suffering from mental illness disorders and cover them up for fear of being "outed." We are petrified we will be stigmatized as crazy and only a step away from Nurse Ratchet overseeing our daily activities. With cancer, though, we feel empathy in a different form and respond in a more hands-on manner.

I kick myself that I was not able to understand Gabe's behavior then, so I now try to be more dialed in and sensitive in his memory. I suppose what I went through could happen to so many of us. There is a stigma associated with mental challenges, regardless of their nature. But no one is immune to these challenges, and we all can do our parts to help the afflicted.

When a member of our community was diagnosed recently with breast cancer, we all jumped into action. Some volunteered to help with her kids' carpools while others took on shopping and household errands. Someone created a Google sign-up sheet for friends to keep her company during chemo treatments and organize meals for the family. As a rabbi, I was proud to see our community respond without missing a beat. It was beautiful, empathetic, humane, and the core of what we do as a place of worship and a people.

I wonder, though, if we would respond the same way if said person were to say she was suffering from depression and could not get out of bed, or she had OCD and was hoarding stuff or perhaps unable to leave the house because she needed to take exactly fourteen steps to get to the front door and she could not get the cadence for that exact walk down. Or if she were afraid to go out of the house for paralyzing fear.

We build walls around mental illnesses to keep ourselves away for fear of catching "it" or being near "it." That only makes the disease more acute for the afflicted and creates a vicious downward spiral for those working toward healing. What causes us to draw near when someone is physically ill and pull away when someone is mentally struggling?

I believe it is time to address the challenge and destigmatize mental illness in our community and recommend four steps to help us do that:

Don't whisper about it. The strides that were achieved by the LGBTQ community came as a result of people being bold enough to come out and share their identity and story. We have embraced breast cancer with pink ribbons, annual walks, and a month of pink end-zones in the NFL. Now we need to 'come out' about mental illness and embrace those who are stricken. Drawing near to those with health challenges and making Google spreadsheets for meals and carpools are no less important for the person suffering from depression as it is for the one receiving chemo. But we all must be able to say in a full-throated manner that we are battling a mental illness and need help, or we are helping someone with a mental illness.

Mental illness needs a ribbon. I am not sure what colors are available. Orange is for gun control, purple for sexual abuse awareness, and yellow for our soldiers and those missing in action. Perhaps gray. It really does not matter as much as being able to wear our awareness on our proverbial sleeve. Let's talk about it more freely and create understanding and support.

Mental illness is not contagious, and we need to stop treating it like the cooties. Do not be afraid to help those in need; get close to them, and be the support they desperately require and will benefit from. Equally important, do not wait to be asked to help. Be proactive. Being present will not cure mental illness any more than carpools cure cancer. But the presence and support matter.

Know the numbers. We are not miracle workers or magicians. We cannot make the disease go away, but we can help. Sometimes the illness needs more resources than a Google spreadsheet can offer. Know the numbers of suicide prevention hotlines. Keep the number of accredited psychiatrists nearby in order to offer support that is beyond our grade of expertise. Do not try and wear a cape or offer simple solutions to solve the problem.

I would do almost anything for another day with my brother. I cannot bring him back. But I can do my part to ensure others do not have to suffer the pain I live with daily. This starts with recognizing the affliction and being supportive in any way we can.

Try these small steps. Make your life and our world a place for all to feel it is worth living in. Together, we can support those with a mental health affliction and bring more awareness to those in need. Let us act before it is too late.

- RABBI DAVID-SETH KIRSHNER

FROM INFERTILITY TO POSTPARTUM BLUES
AND EVERYTHING IN BETWEEN

Jeremy and I were married almost a year when we started trying for a child. I was thirty-two and didn't expect any difficulty. I'd had two unplanned pregnancies that didn't make it in my twenties, and no one in my family had problems conceiving.

My IUD came out in September 2016. I didn't bleed that month. Well into October, I thought, "I'll just pee into a cup and see what happens on a test strip." The line was so faint, I couldn't tell if I was wishing it into existence. But soon after, I started bleeding, going through a tampon an hour. I saw a nurse practitioner, who prescribed progesterone and told me to call back if it didn't stop in a few days. I actually had to ask what had happened. "Was this a period?" Her reply: "Yeah, probably."

Six months later, I went to see my OB, a young woman I'd really liked when I first met her. Scheduling the appointment, I said I wanted to talk about getting pregnant, to see if anything was wrong. When I arrived, the receptionist greeted me: "Oh, right, you're here for an infertility consult."

I felt gut-punched. I hadn't even considered the possibility of "infertility."

When I met with the doctor, she mentioned my weight. Yes, I'm overweight. I've also got an autoimmune disorder; chronic pain; bone defects and scar tissue in my feet; polycystic ovary syndrome (PCOS); and depression, all of which put me on medications that cause weight gain and make it difficult to lose. I'd weaned off all medications for pain and migraines, and one that helped keep my autoimmune flares at bay. But as overweight women know, most doctors will blame your weight for whatever ailment you present—a sprained wrist, a headache, or lack of ovulation.

She wasn't wrong. Complications from PCOS and an ovulation can be worsened considerably by weight and lessened by weight loss. She asked about my diet, and she *liked* my responses. Then she told me to go running every day. Due to multiple surgeries on each of my feet, that's literally impossible. When I explained why I was looking for a different exercise or diet suggestion, she laughed at me. She honestly, frankly, genuinely *laughed*. "Well, how'd you think you'd lose the weight?"

I was stunned. I wanted to scream, "Why on earth do you think I'm here if not for help?"

She referred me to a fertility specialist, told me he'd put me on a diet, and said I should come back once I got pregnant. I never returned.

* * *

Two weeks later, I met a lovely reproductive endocrinologist. He was gentle and kind, and told me I needed to lose twelve pounds before he could assist me medically. We ruled out any male fertility issues.

After sixty days of trendy diets, I was ready. Unfortunately, he was on vacation. I made an appointment for the following month.

* * *

I fell into a depression. I catered for a living and ate what I made. I sat at home, gained weight, lost weight, slept. I canceled the appointment.

Did I waste my opportunities ten years ago? Would it never happen, because now I was fat and would never not be? Had I failed my husband, my faith, my community, my family by ending the pregnancies of an abuser? The dominoes fell. Anything less than perfect was another straw, another weight, another demerit.

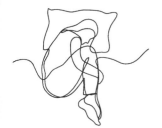 **I fell into a depression.**

As I spiraled downward, the intrusive thoughts began. What would happen if I didn't turn the steering wheel with the curve of this highway ramp? What would I do if Dinah, our dog, ran away? My husband hasn't answered my texts in twenty minutes. Did the dog have a seizure, flip out and maul him to death? Was that chicken defrosting in the fridge for too long? Will we both get food poisoning? If Jeremy dies, can I keep living? Dominoes of disaster.

I'd spiraled before, though never had I felt my only salvation was getting my body to behave. After all, when had my body ever done just what I'd asked of it?

I started a number of projects. I learned about keto for PCOS. I became more active in my religious community. I found hope in the faces of my friends' children, in the tefillot written for women on fertility journeys, in my husband's calm and frank statement: "If it ends up that our family is just you and me, then that will be our family. And I'll be happy."

* * *

In August, my enthusiasm returned. I lost the weight once more and made an appointment with the doctor… who was out of town again. A month later, at an office closer to my home, I met the reproductive endocrinologist of my dreams. He hugged me. He apologized for the mismanagement of my appointments. He looked at the numbers. He looked at *me*. He told me millions of heavier women were able to get pregnant. My womb wasn't empty because of my size.

He wasn't the first doctor to acknowledge my body was more than just fat tissue or to treat me like a person rather than an imbecile. But he was the first to tell me my weight was neither a moral failure nor the cause of my infertility.

He suspected I wasn't ovulating. After a year of trying, if I had ovulated at all, even rarely, I'd be pregnant by now. They started drawing blood daily, which went on for weeks. I tracked my temperature and peed on ovulation-kit strips. He put me on a breast-cancer medication with the side effect of inducing ovulation. Jeremy and I continued to try.

Two months later, he prescribed a "trigger" shot of human chorionic gonadotropin (hCG) around the time the ovulation-induction medication should've been helping my ovaries release an egg. I injected myself on January 7, 2018. I found out I was pregnant two weeks later.

* * *

July 1. I felt some pain. I met my OB-GYN in his office, and in the span of 30 minutes, he went from "Let's check you out; I'm sure you're fine" to "Let's sit down and talk" to "You need to go to the hospital *now*."

I'd thought the massive hemorrhage at eleven weeks was my one big pregnancy drama; before that, the extreme hCG spike that suggested twins. When we made it to the last trimester, I thought all the craziness was over.

We rushed to the hospital. I wish I knew how to convey the humor of all this. I had no idea I was in preterm labor. I figured, "Oh, hospital, that'll take a while. I guess I should bring something to do—my phone, my charger, a book, the water bottle I bring everywhere. What else could I need?"

Once there, my exceptional nurses kept both baby and me alive with compassion, kindness, and generosity. We thwarted my son's impatience for eighteen days, while my loving community visited with meals.

On July 17, Jeremy brought Dinah to visit. I was over-the-moon excited to see her. She, of course, freaked out over everything she saw and smelled, and was too overwhelmed to cuddle. I cried tears of surprising intensity when they left.

The next morning, my daily sunrise stomachache grew too painful to ignore. I called my doula (and best friend) crying, asking if I should bother to wake my husband. My emotions were everywhere. It took me hours to realize I was having a baby *that day*.

With fetal distress, a uterus nowhere near fully extended, and a surprise epidural, it took about six hours and two pushes for three pounds, seven ounces of baby to arrive in this world and into my arms for a precious few minutes before his trip to the NICU.

He was stunning. I was stunned. He looked like an actual baby, not some half-baked baby bird. I made that. I made him. We made him. Adrenaline and oxytocin soared. (Thank you to everyone who lied and promised me he looked just like a regular baby. I needed that.)

When they finally let me see him in the NICU, he was so tiny, in a gigantic preemie diaper, hooked up to tubes and cables in an incubator, under bili lights wearing protective sunglasses.

 **He was actually here.**

The doctors and nurses used terms I'd never heard outside a NICU: "Wimpy white-boy syndrome." "Grower and feeder." "Brain bleed." "Patent ductus arteriosus." "Let's not agitate him by touching him."

We wept. We held each other. We sang to our son. We celebrated. We shook with relief and joy. And nerves. He was actually here.

It took thirty days to settle on his name, fifty-six to see him home. We traveled daily to the NICU and got certified in infant CPR. Our wonderfully generous friends practically moved in to help prepare the house for the baby. I pumped eight to twelve times a day and never managed to produce more than six ounces total. I changed my diet, drank my weight in water, took supplements, suffered five bouts of mastitis. And pumped and pumped and pumped.

Once again, my body couldn't do what I asked of it. It couldn't hold in the baby, for even those eighteen days, without medical intervention. My breasts couldn't nourish him, even *with* medical intervention. My will wasn't strong enough to overcome whatever chemical imbalance prevented me from producing enough milk. Still I pumped.

Eight weeks after he was born, Avishai Lev came home. The adrenaline and tension that pushed us through those two months exploded into elation.

That night, I gave him gripe water drops for the first time for gas. His head flopped back, unresponsive for perhaps five full seconds (Jeremy insists it was much shorter; I stand firm). My life flashed before my eyes, and my CPR training sprang forth. I opened my mouth to scream, and up the baby popped, grunting his vigorous preemie grunt. I cried. He cried. He slept. He grunted.

Two days later, I started crying in earnest and couldn't stop.

* * *

In the eight weeks he lived in the NICU, we didn't stop to consider how it would be to bring him home and be fully responsible for him, to live without the monitors, sensors, alarms, and experts in case something went wrong. We hadn't noticed how noisily he slept or how often they put him on his belly—a no-no at home—to alleviate the pressure on his bowels. He had ridiculous gas from his high-calorie, high-iron formula. The breastmilk he was getting (both the little I produced and that of the beautiful souls who donated theirs) could only help his never-ending digestive distress so much. Still three weeks from his due date, he could not spend any real time awake and was so uncomfortable in his sleep.

By the time of his bris, nine days after he arrived home, I had mastered one way to tie the stretchy cloth carrier, showered twice, and "slept" nine nights on the edge of the bed, my head by Jeremy's feet, my hand on the baby's chest—my version of the heart rate and breathing monitors we'd depended on for his entire short life. I got perhaps twenty minutes of real sleep at a time, a few times a day, and I couldn't speak for crying. I couldn't sleep without watching him breathe. I couldn't see a pregnant woman without flaring up in white-hot rage—at her, her unborn child, at God, at my body, at myself. I couldn't stop imagining some new way I might mess up, injuring or killing my son. Intrusive thoughts crept back into my life: What if he fell, and I caught him in a way that injured him grievously? Could I possibly live if he died? Previous treatment for depression and anxiety had prepared me to expect some form of postpartum blues, but I was not prepared for the rage or the terror.

* * *

Today as I write this, Avishai is fourteen months old. Thanks to our parents, friends, and community, that rage, terror, and anxiety have abated.

My son has grown, changed, teethed, eaten, and giggled his way from a three-pound nothing to a ginormous toddler, crawling, standing, and cruising along the couch. By the time you're reading this, he's probably walking and speaking more words than just "mama." Like everyone said, our hearts have grown in ways we never could've understood. Our lives orbit on a different axis; our marriage is different, stronger, intensely loving. My body, forever a vessel that betrayed me, made this funny, smart, generous, beautiful little creature. I have learned my capacity for love, exhaustion, physical exertion, and cleaning poop out of all kinds of places are greater than I ever could have known.

- MEREDITH SCHWARTZ

MY TRUTH
DISCOVERING WHO I AM

I firmly believe people come into their own truth at their own time. All reality is affected by that. If you grow up in a very conservative family or in a small town where everyone is the same, that's going to affect when you come into your own truth, whether that's straight, gay, trans, or anything else. I came into mine in 2018. But there were moments in my youth when that truth could have emerged. It's one of those hind-sight is twenty-twenty situations.

My truth is, I'm a man. But I was born female. And until June 2018, I lived as a woman with a husband and two children.

I grew up in a family with many women. My mom, aunts, cousins—they were all very second-wave feminist. My mom grew up in the 1950s and 1960s, part of the bra-burning generation. That foundation is important for the feminist movement, but I feel a lot of people are stuck there and never moved forward. The younger generation is more about "it doesn't matter." If you want to wear a dress, wear one. If not, don't. Just don't hurt other people. I hold strongly to that philosophy.

My truth is, I'm a man. But I was born female.

I didn't have a good relationship with my parents, and I resisted everything my mother wanted me to be. I went through phases when I refused to dress femininely. Whenever I wore a t-shirt and wide-legged jeans, she wanted to know why I was dressed like a slob. It was complicated. While I couldn't verbalize it at the time, I guess I was trying to be masculine. One of the questions that come up with the trans narrative is, "Do I not want to be a woman, because I was born in the wrong body and am supposed to be a man, or am I rebelling against the patriarchal system that dictates what a woman is supposed to be?" It's almost a universal struggle with transmasculine people—those who are assigned female at birth but don't identify as women.

But again, I didn't know who I was back then. Growing up in suburban Atlanta in a nonreligious Christian family, I was taught there are people who believe in lots of things, and I should know about them in order to be culturally aware. But I have always had an attraction to Judaism.

I met my husband, who I'll call "Alan," when I was in high school. He's five years older. We started dating when I was a freshman at Wesleyan college in Macon, Georgia, the first college in the world to grant women full degrees just like men could get. I know, ironic. We married in 2010.

Alan is Jewish but not religious. He never had a bar mitzvah. As I got involved with his family and their traditions, I had a lot of questions they couldn't answer. He suggested I find a rabbi, so I did. I met with him regularly, and ended up converting in January 2013 at twenty-four. That same year, our son was born, and I fell into a serious postpartum depression. I had gone from working full time to being a stay-at-home parent to a newborn, which was a pretty rough transition. And because of my relationship with my biological family, the only help I had was from my in-laws.

I felt so isolated and lost. Finally one day, I went to talk to our rabbi. He referred me to Jewish Family & Career Services, and I started seeing one of the social workers. She helped me deal with the combination of feeling isolated, not working, not really having any social life, and trying to find friends who had children my kids' ages (who I got along with). She helped me work through my struggles with my mother and my decision eventually to sever ties with her, which was very traumatic. The last time I talked to any of my family was in 2015—about the same time I became pregnant again.

After my daughter was born, my weekly therapy helped me get through another postpartum depression. We talked about my youth a lot, and as we discussed the childhood traumas I was still dealing with, I started thinking more and more about the role of gender in my life. It was one of those things where you look back and realize something you hadn't before.

I felt so isolated and lost.

I started doing research, reading about people's experiences—both real and through characters in fan fiction. There's a lot more to it, but that's what led me to this moment of self-actualization and self-exploration. What was it I did want? If I could be whatever I wanted, what would it be? If I lived alone on a desert island, what would I wear or do? I spent many months talking to friends and their husbands, asking what life is like being a man. I asked Alan. He is a cis man: He identifies with the gender assigned him at birth. He never questioned it, so verbalizing it was difficult. "Why do you feel like you're a man?" It's hard to answer.

It was very much a gradual realization that became overwhelming. It felt so true, yet it was absolutely terrifying. I hit a point where I couldn't hold it inside any longer and knew I had to talk to Alan about it. He really struggled with it those first few months. It caused some real existential crises. Having always identified as straight, he had to grapple with his love for me—now a man.

Alan grew very frustrated with himself and me, and the whole situation. He had to do a lot of soul searching to come to grips with the understanding that if we stayed together, people were going to think he's gay. Eventually he came to the conclusion it didn't matter, and we started presenting to the world as a gay couple with two children. It was awkward at first. People asked really invasive questions, like "Were your kids adopted?" Should we evade the questions? Tell the truth and out me, that I'm trans? Those are choices we have to make every time we meet people. Today, it's fine. It's normal. We're a family. He comes home from work, and we do family things – make dinner, help kids with homework. He tells people he meets through work he has a husband and has not had many negative reactions.

Today, it's fine. It's normal. We're a family.

As far as I'm aware, I'm the first trans person to go to our synagogue. Every step I take to be a member of that community is a new experience for all of us. Some people know, some don't. Everyone has a different opinion. It was really important that we as a family had the support of the rabbi and staff before we took steps with everyone else.

In early 2019, I began taking testosterone. I changed the gender on my driver's license and passport. I plan to have surgery, but it's expensive and complicated, especially because I have kids. It's hard not to worry about what people might think. But honestly, in the past year, I have found most people don't care. That's how it should be. It shouldn't matter or be a "thing." We have discussions with our kids and with each other about what it means to have a family that's different in any kind of situation. My kids are exposed to a variety of people and relationships, and family dynamics.

Am I happy now? I generally am. I try to look at the world in a positive way, which isn't always possible. I do get depressed, and I continue to have severe anxiety about pretty much everything. It's something I have been working on with my therapist. Medication has helped. It's a process of taking those little steps of being uncomfortable with something, doing it, being terrified, and seeing everything turn out OK.

There are days when I have a crippling dysphoria, which often accompanies depression and anxiety. With any mental health issue, some days people with depression wake up and are fine. Some days, they can't get out of bed. Dysphoria is the same way. Some days I wake up and feel totally confident in myself, and everything is great. Some days I wake up, and everything is terrible and wrong. I'm lucky Alan and our son can walk to the elementary school. I drive our daughter to preschool, and there are days when I have to just throw on a pair of sweatpants and don't get out of the car when I drop her off. Then I go home and curl up on the couch for four hours.

After school, on days when my dysphoria is low, I pick my kids up, and we go somewhere to play and go on outings or various activities. But there are days when I pick the kids up and go home, and the TV goes on until bedtime. It's easier now than when they were babies. It's a continuing journey, but I'm definitely in a better place than I was before. I'm much more comfortable with myself and what I'm doing with my life. I think it's so important to talk about these things. Everyone has those days. People just need to speak up.

- JOSIAH (ALAN'S HUSBAND)

OUR NEW REALITY

The first time we started talking about Josiah transitioning, it was quite dramatic. I could tell something was coming up, and I was pretty sure of the general direction it would go. But I wasn't sure how much of a thing it was going to be.

It was a hard few days to a week of talking and figuring things out—figuring out what it meant for us. I did not react well. I was rude and self-centered. When you care about someone, and you're in a relationship, and they're telling you something deeply personal, and you're taking it and turning it around to be about you, that's very selfish. It might be understandable; many would have reacted the same way. But that doesn't make it right or good.

Look, it's complicated for people who talk about it every day. It's more complicated for people who don't talk about it every day. How can I explain? Josiah was a "he" even from childhood. *When the pronoun came into use is the question.*

Josiah let me go through various stages of denial and understanding. At a basic level, I thought, "OK, so this is the new reality." What does that mean for me? That we're not a family anymore? No. That I want our relationship to end? No. That's why I better accept it. But what does this mean?

I had to come to grips with my own self-image. People have asked me if I'm gay. I'm not. I am "Josiah-sexual." I have an inherent discomfort with being identified as gay. But I think most people who say rude and obnoxious things don't know how they're acting, so I'm able to make fun of them and laugh.

I had to come to grips with my own self-image.

I went through some sadness, although I was never depressed. Depression is chemical. At a basic level, my life didn't really change. I'm in the same relationship with the same person. I'm happy my spouse is doing better than ever. Josiah is an awesome parent to my kids. The hard parts of my life come more from wrestling with career paths and life changes I didn't expect to happen. Or coming to grips with what it means to be a parent and not a toxic male influence.

When one of us needs support, the other gives it.

I'm very pragmatic. I was told reality was going to be different going forward. No negotiation; this is now the reality I have to live in. I came to grips quickly, which is how I generally live my life anyway.

It started with me freaking out in a way I shouldn't have and then realizing that was not the way I should have behaved. I didn't have a choice, so either I wanted it to succeed or end. Never once did I consider leaving. We have a strong relationship. When one of us needs support, the other gives it. If we ever start fighting on a regular basis, we step back. Our job is to be supportive and not adversary. It's not always easy, but it's always right.

- ALAN (JOSIAH'S HUSBAND)

GUILTY HALF SENTENCES

It was 2006. A lifetime ago. The flight home from Israel went by in a daze, and before I knew it, I was standing at the luggage carousel, waiting for my big black suitcase. I already had a suit bag carrying most of my clothes and an overnight bag. For a few moments, I forgot everything and focused on wrestling my baggage from the carousel.

The time had come to face my parents. They would be waiting just through the sliding doors. I could not imagine how I would face them and pretend I was fine and not on the verge of a breakdown. I knew how excited they were to see me. Especially my mom. She had been waiting for me to come home since before I left. Over the past few weeks, I had considered asking her if I could stay, but I knew the question alone would devastate her.

 **The time had come to face my parents.**

My heart trembled, and my head pounded, bringing me back to drunken nights as a teenager. The night I got wasted and told my parents I was depressed as an excuse for my bad behavior. I breathed in deeply and located the way out. I walked briskly, staring straight ahead, my teeth clenched to hold back my emotions.

I spotted them after a few seconds. My father had already seen me, and I saw the dorky smile on his beaming face. He pointed me out to my mother, and I saw her nervous excitement grow. My own face dropped, and tears nearly came flooding from my eyes. I tried to smile, but I might as well have tried to sink through the floor. I found my way to them and stood lifeless as they hugged me and welcomed me home.

I tried to find my voice and share their joy—I promise—but the sadness lay way too deep. They did not know I had lost everything. The country I loved, the yeshiva I loved, all of my friends, and... him. Him especially. I could never tell them that.

I watched my parents' faces change. My dad suddenly looked sad and concerned. My mom, disappointed, angry, and deflated. I had ruined her moment. She looked as if she'd suddenly aged twenty years and been purged of everything but skin.

My dad said I was overwhelmed. That it would take some time to get used to being home. We walked to the parking lot, where he proudly displayed his new Tata Indica. Guilt flooded through my arteries as I tried—I promise I tried—to show any kind of interest. Instead, I flopped inside the car and breathed heavily.

As we finally rolled through familiar streets, I became more despondent. The sight of foliage, like you'd struggle to find throughout Israel, made my insides churn. It was all exactly the same as it was during my past life in this land. This land in which he did not exist. A land in which he could not exist, because if I let him exist, my parents would know the impossible truth.

It *was* impossible. I *could not* be gay. And it was still somehow the truth.

* * *

"He's getting settled now," my mom said, as I scooted around the house, trying to find any sign that I hadn't gone back in time a year. "He's back in familiar surroundings, hey?"

She spoke in the third person, her dejection having turned to pity and concern. I was her nineteen-year-old son, and I would soon show her my love. I just had to get settled in my familiar surroundings.

There could not have been a more inaccurate choice of words than settled. My entire being was in upheaval. I could not accept being back here. I tried—I swear I tried. I could not accept what I had lost.

Getting settled. No. Agitated would have been accurate, a word that perfectly described the conflict within me of being in a world both post-him and somehow pre-him. Living in the horror of grieving for someone who never was.

"Can I phone someone…there?" I said, unable to stop myself. My parents looked at each other.

"Okay," my dad said. "Just don't be too long."

I used the landline to call his cell phone. "You're already back?" he said. "Yes," I choked.

"Jeez. I'm sorry."

"Everything is the same as it used to be. I just want to be back." With you.

We had never really discussed our emotions. Our relationship had always been a happy-go-lucky slew of insults, affection, and jokes. This call could only last a few minutes. Neither of us knew what to say, and when I hung up, I felt worse than I had before.

I attempted another route back to the Holy Land. Dovi B. had put together a video of the guys from our program. It was really just a slideshow, scored with songs each of us liked, burned to a DVD.

I told my parents I wanted to watch it. We went to the playroom, which had long ago become the living room in all but name. I started the DVD and watched as the faces of my friends went by. I saw myself smiling, happier than I had ever been, as *Nothing Else Matters* mournfully played.

He went by in bad photos that belied his vitality and charm. I looked at my parents. Neither was watching.

* * *

I lay down in bed at around nine o'clock, believing I would somehow fall asleep and end this long day. Misery flooded my body. Depression overwhelmed me, and I stood up, thinking that would make it better. Standing up did not help. Lying down or standing up, I could not bear this hell. Not for another moment. I could not be in this dark room, alone with my terrible thoughts and burning memories.

I went back to the playroom. My parents were still up, eating dinner while watching Little Britain on BBC Prime.

"I can't sleep," I managed to choke out. My dad nodded, a serious but nonjudgmental look on his face. My mom just stared at the TV. Bed was better. I retired to my room, paced back and forth, returned to the playroom, and sat all alone on the couch as my parents ate dinner a couple of meters away.

There was no solution. I could see that. I had no way of ever getting back to him. Even if I did, what would I do? Tell him I loved him and wanted to be with him? How could that do anything other than make it worse? If there was the slightest chance he felt the same, we would simply both be in the same leaking boat.

I wanted to talk about him. I wanted to tell someone how much I loved him. To detail every little thing that made me crave him. The way he would squeeze my cheek affectionately, the way he would lick my fingers while I did the same to him. The way he called me "Sparky" after I started voicing more of my cutting, cynical humor. He had brought that out in me. He had somehow made it so much easier to express myself. He had made it so much easier to be me.

Talking about him would make it possible to continue what I had started with him. It would mean I wasn't leaving everything I loved about myself with the boy I loved in Israel. It would provide an escape from the serious, reserved, shy person I had always been back home. I needed to talk about him. I knew that not doing so would be catastrophic for my sense of self.

But doing so would destroy my life. I did the only thing I could and remained silent.

* * *

I was depressed. Not a major, agitation-filled "episode" like I would experience later in life and like I had experienced that first night, but a constant inability to smile or enjoy life that led me to believe I had to somehow get back. I told my parents I wanted to emigrate, to make aliyah.

"If you can't be happy in my home, why am I alive?" my mom said. "I should just kill myself."

 # I did the only thing I could and remained silent.

My guilty lips trembled, unable to form a response. Unable to reassure her and tell her it was not her fault, and I could not be happy no matter how hard I tried.

"It's like he's in love with a girl there," my dad said, sometime later.

I would wake up every day at around five o'clock and lie in bed vaguely panicked with the near-certain knowledge I would not make it back to Israel in time. He was only there for another year. After that, there was just no point.

My father was an Israeli citizen, and if I spent more time there, I'd be forced to go to the army. My only option, as I saw it, was to voluntarily emigrate and do the hesder program—another year in yeshiva, after which I'd spend a year and a half in the army. I would have to get back there by May if I was to start the program while he still lived there. No one else understood how urgent this was.

I wondered if there would ever be a day when I did not think about him. I wondered if I could bear the possibility. I needed to get back. I set the wheels turning.

* * *

Getting things done had never been my strong point. And now I had to organize my emigration all by myself. It was impossible, I knew. I did not have a driver's license. I had no money. I had very little information. Still, I did not give up. I did not speak of it with my mother except in guilty half sentences. I felt my dad supported it to an extent, but he would not openly back it. I stopped speaking to my parents. I stopped being miserable around them. I showed them no sadness. I showed them no anger. I showed them none of my existential terror. I showed them nothing but numbness.

When, after three or four months, I began to feel happy once in a while, I did not show them that either. They might think my resolve had changed. They might expect me to start talking. To say things I had no will to say. I showed them nothing.

I immersed myself in a South African yeshiva and moved into a flat there. I shut my parents out, visiting for an hour or so on a Friday afternoon and staying every fourth Shabbat. I could never be happy in that home, nor could I be sad or angry. I could only be numb. I dreaded those visits and could not wait to get back to the yeshiva, feeling immense relief on Sunday mornings. Holidays were the same. I stayed away from my parents' home, even when I had to be physically present.

Over time, I stopped talking about returning to Israel. I couldn't overcome the logistical challenges on my own. More important, I had begrudgingly accepted that I was happy in the yeshiva. I felt like I belonged among the kind, lovable friends I had made. I could see the futility of giving that up for a few months with a boy I could never love in the way I wanted.

That acceptance did not in any way alter the way I saw my parents' home. It was my past life. A world in which my new reality did not exist. A world of silence that could never be reclaimed, even when I left religion and came out five years later at the age of twenty-four.

JOSHUA MARCUS

The story been edited from its original version shared on thequeerjew.com.

COURAGE, HONESTY, AND HOPE

With addiction, depression, anxiety, and other mental health challenges soaring among our nation's youth, why are we still afraid to talk about mental health? Why are so many parents refusing to acknowledge these problems and get their kids help? If—God forbid—a family member had cancer, diabetes, or any other disease, wouldn't we do everything we could to address it? We need to give people the permission and courage to seek help. No one should suffer in silence alone. The issues of mental health and substance abuse need a voice.

To be honest, when I first experienced my daughter's anxiety, I only confided in my closest friends. I didn't even tell my mother; I didn't want to worry her. I thought people would see my daughter's struggles as a reflection of my husband and me. I also didn't want people to change their opinion of her. I was afraid her suffering would somehow mar who they thought she was.

Paige was diagnosed with separation anxiety in seventh grade. She had trouble going anywhere without me. I often had to push her out the door to go to dance class or leave her on the sidewalk at Hebrew school. I was told she had to fight through the anxious feelings in order to overcome them. It was heartbreaking to watch her suffer. She often couldn't go to school or would go and end up in the guidance counselor's office. I sought the best therapists and psychiatrists, got her medicated and in therapy, and started to see improvement. In later years, her anxiety became more generalized, and she had bouts with depression. Recently, she was diagnosed with a binge eating disorder. Depression and binge eating are strongly linked; in 2010, the American Psychiatric Association officially defined binge eating disorder as a mental illness. Many people binge eat from time to time, but it's the frequency and the depth of anguish one feels about it that raises red flags. It's important to note the feelings around and the reasons behind the bingeing. This helps determine if it's time to get help. Paige ended up in an intensive outpatient program.

As she was going through all this, her behavior was awful. She was obstinate, disrespectful, and extremely difficult to manage. Soon the behavioral issues became dominant, and we knew we needed to do something drastic. We enrolled her in a wilderness program. Paige spent seventy-eight days in the mountains with no running water, showers, or toilets. To cook their meals, the girls had to learn to make a fire without anything but sticks. She had to search for a water source and then filter the water to make it suitable for drinking. She slept on the ground in a sleeping bag with no pillow under a tarp she had to put up and take down every two days when they moved locations. She hiked with a hundred-pound pack on her back, sometimes for hours. As grueling as this may seem, she will tell you her time in the woods was the happiest she's ever been. The noise and chaos of the world, the stress of social media, and the social pressures were all gone. She had no choice but to focus on herself and heal. Paige came out of the woods strong, confident, kind, appreciative, and thirty-two pounds lighter. She made the difficult decision to defer college for a year and go to a young adult transitional program. She is there now, doing really well, and we couldn't be prouder.

When Paige's anxiety first emerged, I thought I could manage it myself. I'd smile and hold it together and pretend. As a result, I fell into a depression. Recently I was watching a show in which Tim Robbins plays a dad who's struggling. He described the way he was feeling like this: "At times I feel like there is a pair of invisible hands wrapped around my heart, squeezing so tight that I think it's gonna stop beating. I almost wish it would. But it doesn't. It just keeps beating. And I just keep going." His words took my breath away. I have experienced that kind of anguish and despair. My depression had me feeling as though I was walking through mud. I had a physical pain and heaviness in my body. So when it came time to deal with my oldest son's issues, I made a decision: I was going to be free, hold my head high, get him help, and talk about it honestly. I wasn't going to hide him or what was happening. I refuse to be quiet now. If people don't understand or choose to judge, that's on them. I believe honesty is the gateway to understanding, because we fear what we don't understand. It's important for us to all have experiences outside of our understanding in order to grow as human beings.

I also know the signs aren't always clear. In a million years, I never would have believed my smart, sweet, responsible, organized, amazing son would end up addicted to marijuana and Xanax, and basically passed out in his dorm room almost every day all day in college. Ross was really good at hiding it. He would call me and pretend he was on his way to class. He always said he was doing well in his classes. When I didn't see anything posted in the parent portal, he would say the teacher didn't post grades yet, or many teachers don't use the portal, or it was down. His excuse for not answering my calls at night would be he was up late studying. His excuse for not answering my calls during the day: He was tired from being up late studying. I had no reason to doubt him, but I also was not naïve. I knew he drank and smoked pot in high school but not to the extent I now know. He never came home obliterated or obviously high.

 # I'd smile and hold it together and pretend.

When an addict wants to use, he will do everything in his power to make sure nothing gets in the way. Nothing matters except getting high. The drug of choice is irrelevant. It doesn't matter if your child, friend, or loved one is using meth, alcohol, cocaine, or pot; it's the reason behind why they are using that matters. For my son, it was severe social anxiety and OCD. In other words, mental illness.

Ross called us in February of his freshman year and said he needed to come home. He had not gone to any classes and was failing. At first, we gave him a lot of leeway, because we wanted him to heal. We didn't force school or a job. We wanted to get him help first. We didn't understand what was going on, but we saw he was thin, angry, and defensive. I could barely speak to him, and I cried A LOT. My son had become unrecognizable.

I didn't understand the extent of his drug use until he actually came home. We soon discovered he was getting high in his room and on our roof, staying up all night, and sleeping all day. He went through jobs like water and was not doing anything productive. I decided it was time for rehab, and he went into outpatient treatment three days a week. He got clean, seemed happy again, and went back to college in the fall.

By November, he called to tell us he had relapsed and needed to come home. This time it was worse, and it was apparent he no longer could live in our home and get well. By the time I picked him up at school five days after his call, I had him enrolled in a sober living facility and outpatient treatment. We came home on a Sunday night, and he started on Monday. My friends were in awe, saying things like, "I can't believe you got it all together so fast." "How did you know what to do?" "How did you have the courage to do it?" I had no choice. If I had not done these things, I would have been doing a great disservice to my child. Sometimes as parents, we need to make difficult decisions, because it's what's best. It was one of the hardest, saddest things I have ever had to do, and he hated me for it.

I also know the signs aren't always clear.

Ross spent more than six months sober. He had a job, lived in our home, went on a Birthright trip to Israel, and started full time in college. But then he quit his job and barely attended his classes. He stayed up all night and slept all day, and his OCD was in full force. We had him move into an apartment where he was drug tested weekly. We wanted him to be part of a community where he could have social interaction and accountability. He remained clean but isolated himself and played his video game round the clock. He basically replaced his pot smoking with gaming, and while a much safer addiction to have, it was an addiction nonetheless. According to the World Health Organization, digital games can be addictive, and those addicted to them need help. There are actual mental health programs and tracks dedicated to gaming addiction now. It's considered a clinical impulse control disorder—an addiction in the same sense as compulsive gambling.

I was not going to allow my son to go down the rabbit hole again. We told him he would enter a young adult transitional program, or we would not support him financially. So Ross flew to Utah and began the program. He has a lot of work ahead of him but is feeling happier, sleeping better, and making wonderful social connections.

Then there's my youngest son, who struggles with anxiety. He also has ADHD and a language processing disorder. He's an amazing kid who fights hard to overcome his struggles. He's an incredible soccer player but panics when he has to try out for a new team and gets nervous before games. He runs from situations where he doesn't know what to expect. He has missed out on dances, parties, and other things teenagers love. My husband and I are keenly aware of how his siblings' troubles have affected him. It hasn't been easy for any of us.

We are a family that feels things intensely. Nothing is "wrong" with us. We aren't weird or scary like many with these issues are portrayed on TV. But it can feel like a game of whack-a-mole my house: One issue pops up, another goes away, and I just keep hitting that mole!

My friends often ask me privately for advice, because I'm open about what we've been through. But they swear me to secrecy. Why are they so ashamed?!? Hiding and whispering about these issues is what's shameful. Once I was sitting at lunch with a bunch of friends and realized every girl at the table had a child who was either using my kids' therapist or psychiatrist, or starting meds or a combination of the three. Yet they didn't want each other to know.

I belong to a Facebook group called Grown and Flown. It has 95,000 members from all over the country with children who are grown, in college, or about to launch into the world. Every day there are multiple anonymous posts asking for help or advice in regard to a mental health or substance abuse issue: "I can't post on my own page, so I'm reaching out to this wonderful group." Or "looking for help from my virtual friends, because my real ones won't understand." While it's fantastic for people to have a place to ask for help, when I see one of these anonymous posts, I want to scream WHO ARE YOU AND WHY ARE YOU HIDING?!?

Why are they so ashamed?!?

If you are going through any of what I have described, here's some advice: Take care of yourself. You are no good to anyone if you are a mess. Take walks, go to the gym, get a massage, or just lock yourself in the bathroom for ten minutes and breathe. Force yourself to sit in quiet and not think. Snuggle your dog. Take a bath. Find something that makes you happy. If you are touched by someone struggling with substance abuse, remember the three C's...You didn't CAUSE it, you can't CONTROL it, and you can't CURE it. And when it comes to mental illness, you can't love or parent it out of them. Ask for help. In this social media age of FAKEBOOK, Insta-feel-bad, Snap-a-lie, and endless selfies, be the person who spreads honesty. Be the one who lends a compassionate ear without judgement. But mostly, TALK and don't stop. You are not alone, and together we can quiet the silence.

- MARCI TALARICO

RESOURCES

The following pages offer additional support and insight. If you need further assistance, we encourage you to contact a local therapist or medical professional.

- Self-Care
- Gratitude & Joy
- Jewish Prayers for Healing
- National Mental Health & Addiction Hotlines
- Mental Health Glossary

SELF-CARE

What is self-care? It's different for everyone, and it can be categorized into several buckets, including emotional, physical, mental, social, and spiritual. Only an individual can decide on the type of self-care needed and the frequency in which he or she needs it. And even if you think you don't need it, trust us; you do. Nothing is more important than taking care of yourself.

The first step to creating a self-care practice is to get more in touch with your personal needs and interests. Taking care of yourself doesn't have to mean massages and manicures, or a round of golf. In fact, it doesn't have to require a lot of money or time. In most cases, the best self-care practices cost nothing.

Self-care doesn't have to be something you're good at. It can be something you're interested in learning or accomplishing. Setting a new goal and accomplishing it are great examples of self-care.

Self-care is preventative and interventional. If you regularly take time to practice it, you're acting to prevent stress. If you have a high stress level, it's important to begin self-care practices as intervention.

Self-care comprises two ideas: intention + time.

Intention

If you don't know where to begin, ask yourself this: "If I had free time with zero obligations for a day, what would I do? How would I spend my time?"

Everyone is going to have a different answer. The key is to be intentional about how you spend your time. You choose to do something because of how it makes you feel. Recognizing the effect of the experience, and knowing the feeling came from your self-care practice, solidifies the intention and sets you up for success.

Time

A little self-care is better than none at all. Starting small will create momentum that results in progress. It may mean taking just ten minutes a day to begin creating your self-care practice.

It can be hard to find the time. Life is busy, and individuals are pulled in a hundred ways. The key here is to *make* the time and change your mindset to include self-care in your daily (or weekly) routine.

When you use time and intention in your self-care practice, you'll find your mind will be clearer, and you'll feel more relaxed and re-energized.

As your self-care practice deepens and becomes more routine, the next step is to encourage others in your community to create their own self-care practices. By helping them make positive changes in their lives, you can make a real impact on the world. That's what *tikkun olam* is all about, and there is no better feeling.

Judaism's Connection to Self-Care

The Jewish people were given the gift of Shabbat. That's twenty-five hours when you can press the pause button and think about you. A time to share with the people in your community and to nourish your body and mind. Shabbat may look traditional with the authentic meals and prayers, or it can be something unique you create. It brings intention to your life, allows you to set aside time in your busy day, and pushes you to put yourself first.

Take this idea of time and intention, and disperse it to other parts of your week. It doesn't matter what you do to care for yourself, as long as it is a boundary you create for yourself and is surrounded by intention.

Self-care practiced routinely will become part of your personal ritual. It will grow from something you attempt to do regularly into something you don't think about doing. And it will change your life before you know it.

A Self-Care Story

Beth Ricanati, MD, FACP, is a physician, mother, and author. She shares her self-care ritual, as adapted from her book Braided: A Journey of a Thousand Challahs:

I made challah once, because a friend suggested I try it. I have kept making challah for more than ten years now, with 1,000-plus challahs (and have even written a book about my journey!), because I felt better from it. Because the countless demands on my time and energy overwhelmed me, literally and figuratively, and getting my hands sticky in a bowl of dough helped. Because as a physician I know all too well that stress like this makes us sick—not just theoretically sick, but actually sick.

Through this repetitive weekly activity of making homemade bread, either alone or with others, I have come to appreciate a simple way to manage my stress. Making bread has become part of my quest for a healthy lifestyle. I have learned I can stop and breathe while I crack eggs, measure flour, and watch the yeast bubble. I can stop and create something with my own hands. In the process, I reconnect with myself and others. In doing so, I have found how to be present.

Stress management comes in all shapes and sizes. Maybe it's baking, gardening, or knitting that engages you. What matters for a healthy life is that you manage your stress so it doesn't manage you. Something that gets you out of your head, that forces you to stop. To be present. To use your hands. To be accountable.

Getting Started with Self-Care

The following is not a fully encompassing list of self-care practices but rather some suggestions for starting off. Always begin with time and intention. Challenge yourself to create a self-care practice that doesn't cost money; the reward is even greater.

- Be social

  ▸ Make plans with friends or family.

  ▸ Join a new social club or group.

  ▸ Attend a community event.

- Get organized

  ▸ Create an achievable to-do list each day that will help you feel accomplished and not overwhelmed or lost. Keep it simple and realistic.

  ▸ Plan your meals for the week to reduce stress around what you're going to eat and to ensure you're eating a healthy diet.

  ▸ Say no. If you're swamped or don't want to go to something, then don't. You have limited time each day and week. It's OK to say no.

- Move Your Body

  ▸ Open your mind, and increase your health through physical activity

  ▸ Try a new exercise, sport, or other pastime.

  ▸ Take a dance class.

  ▸ Walk your dog as often as you can for at least fifteen minutes. It will be good for both of you!

  ▸ Visit a local park for a picnic.

- Reflect

  ▸ Write in a journal. This will help you reflect on how you are spending your time and what is happening in your day.

  ▸ Compose a list of the most important things and people in your life. Reference this list weekly to remind yourself to spend time on these things or with these people.

- ▸ Watch YouTube videos, read books, or research the topic of mindfulness.

- ▸ Challenge your mind with Sudoku or other brain puzzles.

- Relax

  - ▸ Meditate.

  - ▸ Get adequate sleep.

  - ▸ Try cooking or baking.

  - ▸ Find a creative outlet. Try coloring, listening to music, writing, reading a book.

- Treat Yourself

  - ▸ Take yourself out to a nice meal.

  - ▸ Spend money doing something you wouldn't normally do.

This self-care section was compiled by Daniel Epstein, psychotherapist, and Gabby Spatt, executive director of the Blue Dove Foundation.

GRATITUDE & JOY

It's easy to see the connection between gratitude and joy. Let's start with the definition of gratitude: a feeling of thankfulness or appreciation. The feeling becomes magnified when there is intention and awareness. Going further, when you experience appreciation and gratitude, you feel joy.

Joy comes from adding something pleasurable or removing something uncomfortable. The feeling of Joy is the release of dopamine, the chemical that allows you to experience pleasure. It helps regulate movement, attention, learning, and emotional responses. It also enables us not only to see rewards but to take action to move toward them.

A Gratitude Story

Sally Mundell is an author, a philanthropist, a speaker, an innovator, an e-commerce and direct marketing strategist, and the founder of ThePackagedGood.org. Sally also runs You Do Jew, which celebrates all things Jewish and helps people cultivate their "Jew-rney" to a life of meaning, learning, growing, and giving. Learn more about Sally at SallyMundell.com, and follow @YouDoJew on Facebook and Instagram.

MY SECRET SWITCH

Our minds and bodies are capable of miraculous things, one of which I call the "switch." Over the years, I've discovered its power in the seemingly instant ability to shut off my ego and turn on my being. We all can almost instantaneously make the leap from tense and stressed to relaxed, peaceful, and even elated, as evidenced by postcoital bliss.

And while history's best poets have tried to put words to such a seismic shift in feeling, it has proved to be elusive. I think that's because it's an energy shift that transforms not only our way of thinking but also our way of being.

I'm no poet, but I'm going to try and share my transformative experience with what I call the "gratitude switch." With a quick flip, it can power your presence of mind, open your eyes to miracles, fuel your sense of vitality, and bring on your being in the truest sense. Basically, it's a happy switch.

I wasn't seeking this switch; rather, it was sort of forced upon me. And for that, I'm grateful.

I lost my husband, Grover, suddenly to lung disease six years ago and knew if I didn't grab a hold of hope and gratitude, I'd be a goner. I'm not sure why, but one Sunday morning I woke up with my senses tuned into the good going on around me. Even in the midst of tremendous loss and sadness, I smelled the sweet scent of lilies; noticed the kindness of family, friends, and neighbors; and felt excited and appreciative about a promotion at work. The cumulative effect of each small moment of gratitude catapulted me from a numb state of grief to one full of life, happiness, and hope.

At the time, and even to this day, I'm not sure what flipped the switch, but I found it to be self-fulfilling. The more I looked for the positive, the more I saw it. The more I sought reasons to be grateful, the more reasons I found. And while I wish I could say I've been able to stay in this happy place continuously, that's not the case. Without a concerted effort to practice gratitude, the feeling proved to be fleeting, and my mind had a tendency to flip back to the darkness.

I recently finished building a new house, and over the year it took to finish it, I took note of every single issue. From the dysfunctional plans to the missed paint spots to the cracked bathroom tiles, I sent myself into a spiral of exhaustion trying to identify and fix every flaw. One night after my daughters and I moved in, I sat down, took a deep breath, and wondered why, with this amazing new home, I still felt so down.

And then the lights came on. I remembered the power of the gratitude switch and decided to quickly turn it on. And with an actual verbal promise to myself, I started looking for the good. I admired my house's beauty and each of the features I was so excited to have, like my big bathroom with a soaker tub, my walk-in closet with more room than I need, and my walk-out back deck that brings the outdoors in. I decided to write the list of imperfections down on a piece of notebook paper under the title "to be fixed" and at that point removed them from my mind, so they no longer could block me from my being or from my immense gratitude for what I had. I flipped the switch, and just like that, my house became my dream home. I was present. I was alive. I was grateful.

Just a few days after the start of my love affair with my house, I found myself in a familiar pattern with my girls. Frustrated with the backtalk and misbehavior, I was fixating on their faults. I made a mental list of all of the things they forgot to do or didn't do right and started down the self-deprecating swirl of questioning my parenting ability. But luckily before the flush, I caught myself and said "stop." I turned the switch and focused on their compassionate acts of kindness. The love they show each other and our dog, Puff, even if it's sandwiched between some dramatic sisterly fights. I admired their curiosity and creativity, and an abundance of unconditional love for my smart, sweet, amazing girls came flooding through my heart, where it was once dammed by negativity.

Having experienced the power to change my life by changing my mindset—and as a curious being—I'm now in pursuit of new switches. And in the meantime, I'm making sure to keep the gratitude light on.

Judaism's Connection to Gratitude

Prayers are found in all aspects of Jewish life, from birth to death. Take a second to look deeper into their meaning. They scream gratitude and joy. On Shabbat and other holidays, for example, we offer our appreciation by blessing God for giving us the Sabbath, wine, bread, and so forth.

Rabbi Geoffrey A. Mitelman, founding director, Sinai and Synapses, shared his thoughts in the article *To Be a Jew Is To Give Thanks—By Definition*, which ran in the Huffington Post on November 26, 2013. *You can read the full version at* https://www.huffpost.com/entry/jewish-thanksgiving_b_4333641.

The Torah tells us of how Leah gave birth to several sons, and when the fourth one was born, she said, "This time, I will give thanks to Adonai," (odeh et Adonai). The root letters of odeh, "I will give thanks," form the basis of the name that Leah chose for her son: Yehudah. From Yehudah, we get the name "Judah." And from "Judah" we get the word "Judaism."

So in the end, our greatest Jewish responsibility is to give thanks, because when we do, we recognize the holy potential of our world and bring more of it into people's lives. And with that potential, when we look—when we really look—for one hundred blessings every day, we can then create even more of those blessings, for ourselves and for our world.

Getting Started with Gratitude

Gratitude is incredibly personal. To practice feeling and expressing gratitude daily, you'll want to try different things and pay close attention to how they make you feel afterward. The end goal is the feeling of joy. This list is not a fully encompassing list of ways to show gratitude, but rather a starting point.

Send a Card to Someone

Sending a hand-written card makes a huge impact. Individuals often assume people in our lives know we're grateful for them. But many of them don't. If you're grateful for someone, let them know by sending a hand-written card. Individuals will acknowledge and appreciate the time you took to think about them, write a note, and mail it.

Create a Gratitude List

Aim for one hundred things. This can be a very daunting task. The trick is to start with broad categories, and then engage your senses to identify the specific items you're grateful for relating to the larger category.

Examples:

Category - My Pet Dog

- I love that my dog is always waiting at the door for me when I get home.
- The soft touch of his head on my lap.
- His excitement when he puts his head out the window.

Category - Saying Hello to a Stranger

- I see the smile and reaction on a stranger's face when I say "hello."
- It makes me smile when the stranger returns the "hello."
- I hope I make people feel special when I acknowledge them.

Start Journaling

Journaling gives you the biggest bang for your buck. If you're feeling stressed out or confused, write down what you're going through and what you're thinking. The more details about a specific topic, the better. Try to stay solution-focused, and consider writing about people rather than things. Start thinking about what life would be like without the people who bring you gratitude and joy, and stop thinking about the things you wish you had.

Journaling challenges you to move your mind from where it is. The act of writing helps you to clear your mind and offers a sense of calmness. With a commitment to journaling, you'll learn more about yourself and how you react to different situations. This will be a chance for you to develop a new perspective and outlook on life.

This gratitude & joy section was compiled by Daniel Epstein, psychotherapist, and Gabby Spatt, executive director of the Blue Dove Foundation.

JEWISH PRAYERS FOR HEALING

Moments for self-care, mindfulness, and mental health are embedded in Jewish tradition. We have regular opportunities within Jewish liturgy to say a mi sheberach, a prayer that seeks complete healing for ourselves and others, and this sense of completeness includes both the soul and the body. Judaism acknowledges a distinction between mental and physical health while treating them on an equal plane, recognizing that both a healthy body and a healthy mind are necessary for human beings to be complete. *(Adapted from the OneTable Mental Health Shabbat Guide, available at* https://onetable.org/mentalhealth*)*

MI SHEBERACH FOR THOSE IN RECOVERY

God, there are those among us who struggle with addiction. We offer this special prayer for those in recovery:

- Mi sheberach, to the one who blesses: May God bless you with the courage to conquer your cravings, the strength to stay far from temptations, and from people who can lead you astray.

- Mi sheberach, to the one who blesses: May God hear the cry of your soul and bless you with the knowledge that you have the power to remake your life, to repair what has been destroyed, to recover what has been lost, to receive all the blessings that have been ignored.

- Mi sheberach, to the one who blesses: When you fall into despair, may God bless you with hope. If you stray from the path of recovery, may God show you how to begin again. May God renew your faith in yourself. May God open your eyes to all the miracles that surround you.

Bless all those who are living in recovery. God, lead them on the path back to life, back to love, and back to You. Amen.

A PRAYER OF HEALING FOR MENTAL ILLNESS

May the One who blessed our ancestors bless all who live with mental illness, our caregivers, families, and friends. May we walk in the footsteps of Jacob, King Saul, Miriam, Hannah, and Naomi, who struggled with dark moods, hopelessness, isolation, and terrors, but survived and led our people. Just as our father, Jacob, spent the night wrestling with an angel and prevailed, may all who live with mental illness be granted the endurance to wrestle with pain and prevail night upon night. Grace us with the faith to know we, like Jacob, may be wounded, shaped, and renamed by this struggle; still we will live on to continue an ever-unfolding, unpredictable path toward healing. May we not be alone on this path but accompanied by our families, friends, caregivers, ancestors, and the Divine Presence. Surround us with loving kindness, grace, and companionship, and spread over us a sukkat shalom—a shelter of peace and wholeness. And let us say: Amen.

© Rabbi Elliot Kukla, 2008

THE BAY AREA JEWISH HEALING CENTER is dedicated to providing Jewish spiritual care to those living with illness, to those caring for the ill, and to the bereaved through direct service, education and training, and information and referral.

OUR JEWISH RECOVERY

BY RABBI ILAN GLAZER

This is the day that God has made—let us be glad and rejoice in it.

The day you were born is the day God decided the world couldn't go on without you any longer.

Your life matters. Your soul matters.
We are more than our wounds, more than our worst deeds.
We are beautiful, vibrant, holy, angels of God.

Recovery has allowed me to find pieces of myself I didn't even know.
Please, wherever you are on your journey, allow yourself the gift of healing.
I know life has its challenges, and I'm sorry for all the pain and suffering we've all had to endure. I do believe, though, that we have a choice in how to respond to that pain. I hope and pray that we can continue using the tools of the program to heal.

May we all know peace.

Rabbi Ilan Glazer is a freelance rabbi and recovery coach based in Silver Spring, Maryland. He is the founder of Our Jewish Recovery, whose mission is to end the shame and stigma of addiction in the Jewish world and to provide resources, trainings, and healing opportunities for all who are affected by the disease of addiction. Rabbi Ilan moderates the Our Jewish Recovery Facebook group, which is a private space that exists to support Jews in recovery and their loved ones and to help individuals find experience, strength, and hope. Please join us! Rabbi Ilan is the author of And God Created Recovery: Jewish Wisdom to Help You Break Free From Your Addiction, Heal Your Wounds, and Unleash Your Inner Freedom, and the host of the Torah of Life Podcast.

NATIONAL HELP HOTLINES

Following are just a few of the many resources available nationally. Each will be able to connect you with local resources to learn more about counseling options, treatment facilities, educational and training opportunities, support groups, and more.

ALCOHOL AND DRUG HELPLINE

1-800-821-4357

24/7 national hotline that provides resources about local alcohol and drug abuse treatment options. Calls are free and confidential.

AL-ANON FAMILY GROUPS (AL-ANON AND ALATEEN)

1-800-344-2666

www.al-anon.org

A support forum where the families and friends of alcoholics can share their experience, strength, and hope in order to solve their common problems.

CHILDHELP NATIONAL CHILD ABUSE HOTLINE

1-800-422-4453

www.www.childhelp.org/hotline

24/7 hotline with professional crisis counselors that offers crisis intervention, information, and referrals to thousands of emergency, social service, and support resources. All calls are confidential.

NATIONAL ALLIANCE ON MENTAL ILLNESS (NAMI)

1-800-950-NAMI (6264)

www.nami.org

The nation's largest grassroots mental health organization dedicated to building better lives for the millions of Americans affected by mental illness.

NATIONAL CENTER FOR ELDER ABUSE (NCEA)

1-855-500-3537

www.ncea.acl.gov

A national resource center dedicated to the prevention of elder mistreatment. Established by the U.S. Administration on Aging (AoA) in 1988 as a national elder abuse resource center, it was granted a permanent home at AoA in the 1992 amendments made to Title II of the Older Americans Act.

NATIONAL EATING DISORDERS ASSOCIATION (NEDA)

1-800-931-2237

www.nationaleatingdisorders.org

The largest nonprofit organization dedicated to supporting individuals and families affected by eating disorders, NEDA serves as a catalyst for prevention, cures, and access to quality care.

The NEDA Helpline (1-800-931-2237) is available Monday-Thursday from 9:00 a.m. to 9:00 p.m. ET and Friday from 9:00 a.m. to 5:00 p.m. ET to provide support, resources, and treatment options for yourself or a loved one.

NATIONAL DOMESTIC VIOLENCE HOTLINE

1-800-799-7233 (SAFE)

www.thehotline.org

Part of the largest nationwide network of programs and expert resources. Visitors to its website can find information about domestic violence, online instructional materials, safety planning, local resources, and ways to support the organization.

NATIONAL DRUG HELPLINE

1-844-289-0879

www.drughelpline.org

24/7 hotline to help those struggling with addiction receive information regarding treatment and recovery. Call for information regarding treatment and recovery.

NATIONAL SUICIDE PREVENTION LIFELINE

1-800-273-8255 (1-800-SUICIDE)

www.suicidepreventionlifeline.org

24/7 hotline for people in distress and their loved ones to access prevention and crisis resources and best practices for professionals. Calls are answered by local crisis lines whenever possible.

NATIONAL TEEN DATING ABUSE HELPLINE

1-866-331-9474 (Text or Talk)

www.loveisrespect.org

24/7 helpline to answer questions about relationships and dating staffed by an advocate trained to offer education, support, and advocacy to those involved in dating abuse relationships as well as concerned friends, siblings, parents, teachers, law enforcement members, and service providers.

POISON CONTROL CENTER

1-800-222-1222

www.poison.org

Free, confidential service that provides support from a poison control professional (including cases involving drugs and/or alcohol).

RAINN (RAPE, ABUSE & INCEST NATIONAL NETWORK)/NATIONAL SEXUAL ASSAULT HOTLINE

1-800-656-4673 (HOPE)

www.rainn.org

The nation's largest antisexual violence organization, RAINN operates the hotline in partnership with more than 1,000 local sexual assault service providers across the country and administers the DoD Safe Helpline for the Department of Defense. RAINN also carries out programs to prevent sexual violence, help survivors, and ensure perpetrators are brought to justice.

SAMHSA'S NATIONAL HELPLINE (SUBSTANCE ABUSE AND MENTAL HEALTH SERVICES ADMINISTRATION)

1-800-662-4357 (HELP)

www.samhsa.gov

24/7 hotline that provides information service for individuals and families facing mental and/or substance use disorders.

VETERANS CRISIS LINE

1-800-273-8255

www.veteranscrisisline.net

A free, confidential resource available to anyone, even if you're not registered with the U.S. Department of Veterans Affairs (VA) or enrolled in VA health care. The caring, qualified responders at the Veterans Crisis Line are specially trained and experienced in helping Veterans of all ages and circumstances.

MENTAL HEALTH GLOSSARY

U.S. Department of Health and Human Services, National Institutes of Health, National Institute of Mental Health. (2019). RAISE Glossary

ANTIDEPRESSANT: Medication used to treat depression and other mood and anxiety disorders.

ANTIPSYCHOTIC: Medication used to treat psychosis.

AUDITORY HALLUCINATIONS: Hearing something that is not real. Hearing voices is an example of auditory hallucinations.

BIPOLAR DISORDER: A disorder that causes severe and unusually high and low shifts in mood, energy and activity levels as well as unusual shifts in the ability to carry out day-to-day tasks. (Also known as manic depression)

CHRONIC: Persisting for a long time or constantly recurring.

CLINICAL TRIAL: A scientific study using human volunteers to look at new ways to prevent, detect, or treat disease. Treatments might be new drugs or new combinations of drugs, new surgical procedures or devices, or new ways to use existing treatments.

COGNITION: Conscious mental activities (such as thinking, communicating, understanding, solving problems, processing information, and remembering) that are associated with gaining knowledge and understanding.

COGNITIVE IMPAIRMENT: Experiencing difficulty with cognition. Examples include having trouble paying attention, thinking clearly, or remembering new information. (Also see cognition)

COGNITIVE REMEDIATION: Training that uses a variety of techniques, including computer exercises and adaptive strategies, to improve cognition This therapy is designed to strengthen the underlying brain functions that help support cognitive skills such as memory, attention, and problem solving.

COGNITIVE BEHAVIORAL THERAPY (CBT): Helps people focus on how to solve their current problems. The therapist helps the patient learn how to identify distorted or unhelpful thinking patterns, recognize and change inaccurate beliefs, relate to others in more positive ways, and change behaviors accordingly.

COGNITIVE BEHAVIORAL THERAPY FOR PSYCHOSIS (CBT-P): Cognitive behavioral therapy that specifically addresses the positive symptoms of psychosis, e.g., hearing voices.

COMMUNITY MENTAL HEALTH SERVICES BLOCK GRANT (CMHBG): Administered by the Substance Abuse and Mental Health Services Administration (SAMHSA), the CMHBG program makes funds available to all fifty states, the District of Columbia, Puerto Rico, the U.S. Virgin Islands, and six Pacific jurisdictions to provide community mental health services.

COMORBIDITY: The existence of two or more illnesses in the same person. These illnesses can be physical or mental.

CONNECTION PROGRAM: One of two coordinated specialty care models that make up the RAISE research project. The RAISE Implementation and Evaluation Study (RAISE-IES) worked with the Connection Program model in their research.

COORDINATED SPECIALTY CARE (CSC) for first episode psychosis: CSC is a type of treatment that uses a team of specialists who work with the client to create a personal treatment plan. The specialists offer psychotherapy, medication management, CSC case management, family education/ support, and supported employment/education, depending on the individual's needs and preferences. The client and the team work together to make treatment decisions, involving family members as much as possible. The RAISE project tested the effectiveness of CSC for people with first episode psychosis.

CSC: See Coordinated Specialty Care.

CSC CASE MANAGER: This member of the CSC treatment team helps clients with problem solving and coordinates social services. The case manager has frequent in-person meetings with the clinician, the client, and the client's family.

CSC TEAM LEADER: This member of the CSC treatment team coordinates the client's treatment, leads weekly team meetings, oversees treatment plans and case review conferences, and develops transitions to and from the CSC program.

DELUSIONS: Beliefs that have no basis in reality.

DEPRESSION: Lack of interest or pleasure in daily activities, sadness, and feelings of worthlessness or excessive guilt that are severe enough to interfere with working, sleeping, studying, eating, and enjoying life.

DUP: See Duration of Untreated Psychosis.

DUAL DIAGNOSIS: Having a mental health disorder and an alcohol or drug problem at the same time.

DURATION OF UNTREATED PSYCHOSIS: The length of time between the beginning of psychotic symptoms and the beginning of antipsychotic treatment.

EARLY INTERVENTION: Diagnosing and treating a mental illness when it first develops.

EARLY TREATMENT PROGRAM (RAISE-ETP): One of the two studies that make up the RAISE research project. RAISE-ETP compares a coordinated specialty care program for first episode psychosis called NAVIGATE to care typically found in community clinics.

ETP: See Early Treatment Program.

EVIDENCE-BASED PRACTICE: Treatments that are supported by clinical research.

FAMILY EDUCATION/SUPPORT: This part of coordinated specialty care teaches family and friends about first episode psychosis and helps them support the client's recovery. Family and friends are involved in the client's treatment as much as possible and as long as it is consistent with the client's wishes.

FEP: See First Episode Psychosis.

FIRST EPISODE PSYCHOSIS: The first time an individual experiences an episode of psychosis. Also see Psychosis.

FIRST EPISODE SCHIZOPHRENIA SPECTRUM: see First Episode Psychosis

HALLUCINATIONS: Hearing, seeing, touching, smelling, or tasting things that are not real.

IMPLEMENTATION AND EVALUATION STUDY (RAISE-IES): One of the two studies that make up the RAISE research project. RAISE-IES evaluated the impact of a coordinated specialty care (CSC) treatment program called the Connection Program. It also developed manuals, tools, and materials that others may use to start their own CSC program.

INPATIENT: Health care treatment for someone who is admitted to a hospital (also see Outpatient).

INTERVENTION: An action intended to help treat or cure a condition.

IRT: See Individual Resiliency Training.

INDIVIDUAL RESILIENCY TRAINING (IRT): One part of the NAVIGATE treatment program (see NAVIGATE). IRT promotes recovery by identifying client strength and resiliency factors, enhancing illness management, and teaching skills to help functional recovery in order to achieve and maintain personal wellness.

LAI: See Long-Acting Injectable (drugs).

LONG-ACTING INJECTABLE (drugs): A shot of medication administered once or twice a month. The shot is an alternative to taking a daily dose of medication.

MANIA: An abnormally elevated or irritable mood. Associated with bipolar disorder.

MANIC DEPRESSION: See Bipolar Disorder.

MOOD DISORDERS: Mental disorders primarily affecting a person's mood.

NAMI: See National Alliance on Mental Illness.

NATIONAL ALLIANCE ON MENTAL ILLNESS (NAMI): The nation's largest grassroots mental health organization. NAMI is one of more than eighty national nonprofit organizations that participate in the NIMH Outreach Partnership Program.

NATIONAL INSTITUTE OF MENTAL HEALTH (NIMH): The lead federal agency for research on mental disorders. NIMH is one of the twenty-seven institutes and centers that make up the National Institutes of Health (NIH), the nation's medical research agency. NIH is part of the U.S. Department of Health and Human Services (HHS).

NAVIGATE: A coordinated specialty care treatment program for people experiencing first episode psychosis. NAVIGATE is a team-based approach of treatment options that include medication management, case management, individual resiliency training, family psychoeducation, and supported employment/education. NAVIGATE is one of the two coordinated specialty care models tested as part of the RAISE research study. The other program is the Connection Program.

NEGATIVE SYMPTOMS: Symptoms of schizophrenia are often classified as positive or negative. Examples of negative symptoms that "take away" from life include social withdrawal, lost interest in life, low energy, emotional flatness, and reduced ability to concentrate and remember. (Also see Positive Symptoms.)

ONTRACKNY: A coordinated specialty care treatment program in New York for youth and young adults experiencing first episode psychosis. OnTrackNY is based on the work of Lisa Dixon and her team on the RAISE Implementation and Evaluation Study (RAISE-IES), part of the RAISE research study.

OUTPATIENT: Health care treatment given to individuals who are not admitted to a hospital. (Also see Inpatient.)

PHARMACOTHERAPY: Medication selection, dosing, and management. Pharmacotherapy for first episode psychosis typically involves a low dose of a single antipsychotic medication and careful monitoring for side effects.

POSITIVE SYMPTOMS: Psychotic symptoms are often classified as positive or negative. Examples of positive symptoms that "add to" a person's experiences include delusions (believing something to be true when it is not) and hallucinations (seeing, hearing, feeling, smelling, or tasting something that is not real). (Also see Negative Symptoms.)

PSYCHOSIS: Used to describe conditions that affect the mind where there has been some loss of contact with reality. When someone becomes ill in this way, it is called a psychotic episode. During a period of psychosis, a person's thoughts and perceptions are disturbed and the individual may have difficulty understanding what is real and what is not. Symptoms of psychosis include delusions (false beliefs) and hallucinations (seeing or hearing things that others do not see or hear). Other symptoms include incoherent or nonsense speech and behavior that is inappropriate for the situation. A person in a psychotic episode may also experience depression, anxiety, sleep problems, social withdrawal, lack of motivation, and difficulty functioning overall.

PSYCHOEDUCATION: Learning about mental illness and ways to communicate, solve problems, and cope.

PSYCHOSOCIAL INTERVENTIONS: Non-medication therapies for people with mental illness and their families. Therapies include psychotherapy, coping skills, training and supported employment and education services.

PSYCHOTHERAPY: Treatment of mental illness by talking about problems rather than by using medication. Treatment for first episode psychosis is based on cognitive behavioral therapy principles and emphasizes resilience training, illness and wellness management, and coping skills. Treatment is tailored to each client's needs.

RAISE: Recovery After an Initial Schizophrenia Episode (RAISE) is a large-scale research initiative that began with two studies examining different aspects of coordinated specialty care (CSC) treatments for people who were experiencing first episode psychosis. One study focused on whether or not the treatment worked. The other project studied the best way for clinics to start using the treatment program. The goal of RAISE was, and is, to help decrease the likelihood of future episodes of psychosis, reduce long-term disability, and help people to get their lives back on track so they can pursue their goals.

RAISE CONNECTION PROGRAM: See Connection Program.

RAISE-ETP PROGRAM: See Early Treatment Program.

RECOVERY: The process by which people with mental illness return or begin to work, learn, and participate in their communities. For some individuals and their families, recovery means the ability to live a fulfilling and productive life.

SAMHSA: Substance Abuse and Mental Health Services Administration (SAMSHA) is the agency within the U.S. Department of Health and Human Services that leads public health efforts to advance the behavioral health of the nation. SAMHSA's mission is to reduce the impact of substance abuse and mental illness on America's communities.

SCHIZOAFFECTIVE DISORDER: A mental condition that causes both a loss of contact with reality (psychosis) and mood problems (depression or mania).

SCHIZOPHRENIA: A severe mental disorder that appears in late adolescence or early adulthood. People with schizophrenia may have hallucinations, delusions, loss of personality, confusion, agitation, social withdrawal, psychosis, and/or extremely odd behavior.

SCHIZOPHRENIFORM DISORDER: Symptoms consistent with Schizophrenia but that last less than six months.

SEE: See Supported Employment/Education.

SUBSTANCE ABUSE AND MENTAL HEALTH SERVICES ADMINISTRATION: See SAMHSA.

SUPPORTED EMPLOYMENT/EDUCATION (SEE): Part of coordinated specialty care, SEE services help clients return to work or school and achieve personal goals. Emphasis is on rapid placement in a work or school setting, combined with coaching and support to ensure success. Learn more at www.hhs.gov.

PERSONAL STORIES: CONTACT INFORMATION

HER HIDDEN STRUGGLE

Gabby Spatt

Executive Director, the Blue Dove Foundation

www.thebluedovefoundation.org

gabby@thebluedovefoundation.org

ME, AN ADDICT?!?

Rabbi Ilan Glazer

www.OurJewishRecovery.com

rabbiilan@ourjewishrecovery.com

Author, And God Created Recovery

Founder, Our Jewish Recovery -

www.facebook.com/groups/OurJewishRecovery

CONFESSIONS OF A DERMATILLOMANIAC

Erin Pirkle

epirkle18@gmail.com

Facebook: Erin Pirkle

Instagram: Epirkle8

PRACTICING 'TIL IT'S PPPERFECT

Joe Alterman

joealtermanmusic.com

joe.alterman@gmail.com

REPAIRING MY PERSONAL WORLD

Elana Ann Fauth

elanafauth@gmail.com

LESSONS LEARNED FROM MY PARENTS
Rabbi Paula Mack Drill
pmdrill@gmail.com
Facebook: Paula Mack-Drill
Instagram: Rabbi_pmd

MY EMOTIONAL ROLLER COASTER
Jacob Aqua
jaquawellness.com
jaquawellness@gmail.com
Facebook: J. Aqua Wellness
Instagram: jaquawellness

LESSONS FROM LOSS
Rabbi David-Seth Kirshner
Kirshner@templeemanu-el.org
Instagram: @Rabbi Kirshner
Twitter: @Rabbi Kirshner

GUILTY HALF SENTENCES
Josh Marcus
www.thequeerjew.com
josh@theempathyhub.com

Made in the USA
Columbia, SC
09 February 2020